GREENLAND EXPEDITION

Where Ice Is Born

Text and Photography © Lonnie Dupre, 2000

Additional photographer credit: Scott Bensen: p. 156; John Hoelscher: pp. 20, 30, 36, 39, (both), 43, 48, 51 (right), 64, 77, 78, 83, 90, 92, 96, 130, 133, 142, 151; Tine Lisby Jensen: p. 104; Paul Markstrom: p. 23; Larry Roepke: pp. 59, 66, 81, 88, 113; Paul Schurke: p. 15; Mike Sharp: pp. 19, 149.

Linoleum block prints by Kelly Dupre
Maps by Joe Fahey
Book design by Russell S. Kuepper

NorthWord Press
5900 Green Oak Drive
Minnetonka, MN 55343
1-800-328-3895

Library of Congress Cataloging-in-Publication Data

Dupre, Lonnie.
    Greenland expedition: where ice is born / Lonnie Dupre.
        p. cm.
    ISBN 1-55971-707-6 (Hard cover)
    1. International Greenland Expedition (1997-1998) 2. Greenland—Description and travel. 3. Dupre, Lonnie—Journeys. I. Title

G743.D87 2000
919.8'204—dc21   99-053333

Printed in Singapore

10 9 8 7 6 5 4 3 2 1

GREENLAND EXPEDITION

Where Ice Is Born

Lonnie Dupre

NorthWord Press

Minnetonka, Minnesota

Looking north, the east Greenland sunset glows over endless drifting ice pans.
The pans move in and out from shore, compressing and separating at the will of the wind, current, and tides.

TABLE OF CONTENTS

FOREWORD

Lonnie Dupre was born with the Spirit of Adventure. What separates him from most people is that he has followed this Spirit. In Lonnie's case this magnetic attraction was in the North. For most of two decades he has been involved in dog sledding, dog packing, canoeing, and kayaking journeys in the Arctic.

His uniqueness lies in that he is a *doer.* And he does it with patience, a smile, and uncompromising persistence.

* * * *

To have a dream is a wonderful thing, but to make the dream your reality is sheer genius.

* * * *

Organizing the Greenland Expedition took as much energy as—if not more than—the actual execution of the plan. For three years I watched Lonnie struggle and overcome the many nagging problems of raising money and getting permissions and logistics together. This is the unseen adventure, the adventure that separates the babbler from the explorer. And then there are the many critics who say the plan is impossible, and the press is often not too kind to individuals attempting daring feats. These are some of the hurdles, and their stresses strengthen you for the big challenge.

There finally comes that moment when you paddle or mush off, leaving the complicated life behind, to face simple survival. Here the instincts take over and the thought processes play second

Evening in southeast Greenland. The rocks seem to come alive, like a prehistoric serpent surfacing at sea.

A calm, early-summer's day with residual snow seated in valleys and headlands left over from the harsh winter.

fiddle, used only when needed. It is the simple life, but where one mistake in cold water and you die quickly.

Lonnie and John's true achievement was the incredible kayak journeys totaling 2,000 miles halfway around Greenland, a route that has never before been even remotely accomplished.

My biggest fear in the Arctic has always been the cold water, and these two men mastered cold water travel. In the mastery is the seeing and the experiencing, and this is what *Greenland Expedition* is all about.

It is a great read of a great adventure, and well illustrated. It is the closest you will ever get from the armchair to your own Greenland Expedition.

Will Steger

Greenland's north beckons the team—dogs and men.

PREFACE

The International Greenland Expedition was first conceived during the summer of 1995, as my wife, Kelly, and I dog-packed 250 miles across Banks Island, retracing Canadian Arctic Explorer Vilhjalmur Stefansson's 1915 journey. My vision was to create an expedition whose principal objective was to travel around Greenland using only traditional modes of arctic travel—dog team and kayak. Through the expedition, I also wanted to contribute to a better understanding of those indigenous cultures which, in the face of an intruding "civilized" world, strive to retain a traditional way of life based on a balance with nature.

The project was planned as a 15-month, 4,800-mile, non-motorized challenge that would accomplish the first-ever circumnavigation of the world's largest island. It would also provide a unique opportunity to educate people throughout the world regarding the past, present, and future of Greenland. The expedition would be a two-fold project—the adventure of the expedition itself with its related photographic and video documentation, and a concurrent educational program. Kelly, a professional educator and classroom teacher, would function as coordinator for the educational program.

Our budget for this expedition was a modest $400,000. This figure includes donated equipment, in-kind donations, services, and cash. The cash required turned out to be about half of the total amount. It took 26 months to plan, organize, and fund the project. We managed this through some 80 sponsors ranging from individuals to corporations. And it wasn't until just two months prior to our departure that we actually had sufficient funding to start.

The end of a polar night marked the start of our dog sledge journey. Running in the fan formation, the dogs eagerly pull John and our cargo with ease from their 18-foot traces across the flat fjord ice.

At the end of a long day, John removes the uncomfortable dry suit that protects us from hypothermia and death should we end up in the icy water.
We always secured our camp and kayak far away from the waterline when we could. This was to guard against the potential catastrophe of a tidal wave from an
iceberg at sea calving a house-size piece, thus washing everything we have into the ocean.

Putting together an expedition on this scale stretches one's financial neck (and dignity) as far as it can go. Most people are not willing to make those sacrifices. They think the return isn't worth it. But for me, it is. There are risks—physical, emotional, and financial. But working hard, keeping focused, and believing in myself, I was always confident that it would happen in time—one way or the other.

* * * *

So what motivates me to live with the Inuit and travel by kayak and dog sledge in the High Arctic for 15 months? As long as I can remember, I've always been interested in what was around the next corner. I was raised on a Minnesota country farm and, as a child, roamed freely, exploring the nearby woods and swamp. We lived a lot on what we grew or raised on the farm, or what my father brought home from hunting and fishing. I soon learned to hunt and fish as well. Our modest means and farm lifestyle dictated a self-sufficiency that I embraced early. I also became fascinated with the wildlife I encountered while exploring the countryside. I often wondered if there were still people that subsisted on hunting, fishing, and gathering. Later in life, these experiences helped me to understand and admire the ways of the Inuit. Being raised in Minnesota, I also became accustomed to the cold at a young age. I disliked sweating and the heat seemed to give me headaches. I am truly, as a friend of mine put it, a soft candle.

As a family we would always go "up north" to a Minnesota lake for holiday vacations, usually relaxing and fishing. On our way, I wondered just how far "north" went. Were there people who lived up there? How did they handle the cold? I eventually started reading all the material I could get my hands on pertaining to the Inuit (Eskimos) and the Arctic. With my first trip to the Arctic of Alaska in 1983 at the age of twenty-two, I was hooked. I wondered then how I could see and experience the whole Arctic—the environment and its people; not just the villages, but the vast lands of the caribou, polar bear, and muskox. I concluded that the best way was by traditional methods of dog sledging and kayaking.

I confess that the spirit of adventure is strong in me. I easily become bored with everyday life. I often long to step back in time, back to the Arctic where life is a bit less complicated and the basic necessities do not include a late-model car. I love to travel silently with only the sound of dogs' feet hitting the snow and the sliding of the sledge runners. For me, the adventure is in a kayak paddle breaking the surface of glass-flat water on a majestic fjord that has rarely been visited. Seeing new things around each cape, over each hill, or beyond each piece of pack ice keeps me going forward and interested. This is the adventure. After all, isn't life's process supposed to be an adventure?

The expedition around Greenland by dog sledge and kayak epitomizes the human spirit of adventure, and represents an incredible test of individual will. When combined with the other objectives of the project, the expedition became much more than a saga of humans pitted against nature and the elements. It offered opportunities to learn about our planet, our fellow inhabitants, and ourselves.

Lonnie Dupre
November 1999

INTRODUCTION

During a cold and rainy September in 1995 I made the first step in organizing the expedition when I traveled to Denmark to obtain information on maps and to discuss the project with Hauge Anderson of the Danish Polar Center (DPC) in Copenhagen. The DPC is in charge of permits for expeditions seeking to enter the immense restricted preserve that includes most of northern Greenland, as well as for any travel on the inland ice cap. I also met with former members of the Sirius Patrol (a Danish military elite force established in the 1940s that patrols sections of north and east Greenland by dog team) about equipment and route logistics. Greenland had been under Danish rule until 1978, when Greenlanders and Danes both voted for independence and the subsequent establishment of home rule.

Returning to Minnesota, I had my work cut out

for me. I contacted Gary Atwood, a good friend with a talent for writing and organizing, to help with the overwhelming logistics and paperwork. Together we started to develop a fund-raising strategy, sponsorship materials, and a master list of objectives that culminated with the start of the expedition. Over the next few months some 600 letters were drafted and sent out to corporations and organizations that we felt might be interested in coming on board with financial support or in-kind contributions of products or services. Meanwhile, I worked to develop and refine an expedition plan based on my previous expeditions that would offer us the best chance for success.

Keeping alive and traveling in the remote parts of the Arctic is an expensive proposition. We could not afford to use anything less than the best equipment—designed for and tested in the extreme conditions that

During the 1989 Bering Bridge expedition, I comforted my frightened dogs while a Russian helicopter landed on the sea ice separating Siberia and Alaska.

we would encounter. Even then, much had to be modified to meet the standards of performance we would demand. Any donated equipment was much appreciated.

In the beginning, the administrative side of the expedition was supported by my carpentry business in Grand Marais, Minnesota. Then some small donations started to come in through fund-raisers like chili dinners and slide shows. We sold T-shirts, posters, and hats to cover huge phone bills and postage as we contacted hundreds of potential sponsors. Our small house served to store the ongoing mountain of supplies we were accumulating, and the basement became a workshop for modification of the kayaks and building of the dog sledge, which is significantly different from the commonly recognized dog "sled." (The sledge is much larger, varying in length from 12 to 16 feet, and is designed to haul heavy cargo for extended journeys.)

The living room of the house gave way to a maze of desks, office equipment, and boxes of supplies. With the continuous stream of phone calls, deliveries, and expedition activity, and the comings and goings of friends and supporters, the little house was soon referred to around town, with both humor and pride, as the "explorers club." It proved to be a perfect place to organize and mount an expedition.

I had always believed that a small expedition team consisting of two or four individuals was best suited for long and difficult dog sledge and ski expeditions in the Arctic. I soon realized that the length and duration of the project, combined with the mounting costs, would dictate that this be a two-person expedition. In order to successfully travel 4,800 miles in the available time, we needed to travel fast and efficiently. We also knew it was a dangerous undertaking, and would have to keep safety a foremost consideration.

My partner for the expedition, John Hoelscher (born in 1963) from Australia, came on board in September of 1996 to help with preparations. He was a welcome sight with his red hair and "Aussie" mannerisms. The work load had become overwhelming for me with lists upon lists and a rapidly filling calendar. John took over the giant task of dealing with the office and communications.

I first met John Hoelscher when he was delivering some sledge dogs from Antarctica to their new home in Minnesota. John's a native of Queensland, Australia, and had spent a number of seasons in Antarctica at Mawsom Research Station with A.N.A.R.E. (Australia National Antarctic Research Expedition). It was there that he had come to love traveling by dog team. I realized quickly that he would make an outstanding partner in some future endeavor. He was a seasoned and tested man of the polar regions and demonstrated a competent maturity that would serve us well under the rigors of arctic travel. He was also unattached, which allowed him a freedom that is difficult to manage with family responsibilities. His easygoing attitude and love of arctic travel were readily apparent, and as we got to know each other, it became clear that his careful attention to detail would be a perfect complement to my sometimes "big picture" approach. We would test each other's patience at times, but that first meeting developed into a long-term friendship.

With John's participation, we were quickly able to finalize a basic expedition plan. Although it would continue to evolve as we made alterations to accommodate new information and overcome new obstacles, the objective remained fixed—to circumnavigate Greenland using traditional Inuit methods.

* * * *

The attempt would take place between May 1997 and September 1998. It would begin at the settlement of Paamiut, located on the southwest coast. The plan called for a mid-May departure in two 17-foot kayaks. These crafts, specially designed for Greenland's west coast, were constructed of polyethylene and would withstand the punishment of sea ice. The kayaks were capable of being catamaranned together which gave us added stability in rough seas and long, hazardous, open-sea crossings. Before the conclusion of the first kayak leg, this added safety factor saved our lives on at least two occasions. The crafts could also be fitted with small masts and sails to take advantage of any favorable winds.

From the settlement of Paamiut we would travel 1,500 miles north by kayak along the coastal fjords and villages throughout the summer of 1997. We would resupply in the villages along the way and, ice permitting, hoped to reach Qaanaaq in north Greenland by early fall before autumn storms arrived. We would then prepare for the long dog sledging journey by spending five months training and living among the Polar Inuit. We would purchase sledge dogs in the Qaanaaq area and train there with them, all the while gaining a better understanding of the Polar Inuit way of life and gathering information for our educational program.

During preparations, a series of thirteen supply depots would be laid by air and icebreaker along the extreme northern, northeastern, and eastern parts of the island. These are virtually uninhabited areas and offered no other opportunity for resupply during the expedition's second stage—the dog sledge campaign.

With the arctic winter and the sea ice well established, we planned to head north at the end of polar night by ski and dog team, traveling along the northwestern and northern coasts of Greenland and then down the east coast to cover 2,600 miles to the settlement of Ammassalik. We knew we could expect arctic winter storms, with winds reaching 100 miles per hour, temperatures as low as -60 degrees Fahrenheit. Along the route, traveling parallel to the coast, we might also be forced to go high up onto the Greenland ice cap to skirt heavily crevassed areas and to avoid impassable chaotic sea ice.

The expedition sledge, built on a modified traditional komatik design, would be pulled by a team of Inuit "Eskimo" dogs. These dogs are a hardy breed, with an average weight of 75 pounds. Insulated by their heavy fur, they have the necessary endurance and temperament to successfully travel in the extreme conditions of the Arctic.

In the spring, with the sea ice melting and the coastal pack ice breaking up, we would switch to our 19-foot, tandem kayak in the village of Ammassalik. In anticipation of uncertain ice conditions, we chose this durable plastic kayak for hauling across pack-ice when open water is scarce. The tandem kayak was also fast and stable. The first 518 miles of this 930-mile, third and final stage are desolate, uninhabited coast. All supplies for that period would have to be carried in our kayak with no chance of outside help.

Continuing on, we would round the southern tip of Greenland and head north again, completing the expedition at our starting point of Paamiut in August 1998.

We planned to travel during the dog sledge and kayak campaigns an average of 7 to 12 hours per day, and cover an average of 18 miles.

On a regular basis, our expedition would give updates and send out digital photographs from the trail using a laptop computer in support of our educational program, which we would accomplish using satellite communications technology.

The mind-numbing logistics of attempting a contiguous 4,800-mile clockwise circumnavigation of the island left our office struggling to solve the many problems that arose over the shipping of supplies, permits, and route. The transport of supplies to Greenland by ship can only reach certain areas around the coast during the short peak of arctic summer when ice permits. It was a lesson in foreign diplomacy when dealing with officials to obtain all the necessary permits and access to Greenland's northern restricted Preserve. We would be the first expedition allowed to travel through the entire preserve.

We had to modify the route at least a dozen times, changing plans because of the difficulties in selecting a starting point for the expedition that offered the best chance of success. Because of the enormous length of the journey our team had to start and end each leg of the journey during the extreme parts of the seasons. For each kayaking leg we needed to start early in the summer when there was still winter's dangerous sea ice blocking our route. At the other end, either of the kayak journeys could be forced to stop early by the onset of autumn storms, or by the always present ice pack, shifting and blocking our route at the will of the wind and current. As for our dog sledge trek, it was critical that we begin early during polar night and bitter cold temperatures to cover the entire 2,500 miles before summer melted the sea ice out from under our sledge, leaving us and our dogs swimming in ice water to the finish.

If we didn't leave from the right place at the right time, and travel in a clockwise direction around the island, the expedition would fail before it even began. It wasn't until fifteen days prior to reaching Greenland that we confirmed a definite starting point.

* * * *

Northern Minnesota and Lake Superior offered a perfect place to train and test our modified kayaks. The lake, right outside our office door, was always cold and well known for the challenges that made it as dangerous and forbidding as most arctic places. During the winter months we would cross-country ski on the area's frozen rivers and lakes before and after "office hours." Our main training came during the coldest three weeks of the year when we camped and traveled by dog team and ski. A week was spent in the Boundary Waters Canoe Area (BWCA) in Minnesota and two weeks at Lake Nipigon, Ontario, Canada, a four-hour drive from home. Because of the vastness of this lake, it provided conditions similar to those of the Arctic, with driving winds, low temperatures, and hard-packed snow. Here we could train with my dogs in Inuit fashion, running the team in a fan-shaped formation with each of the dogs attached to its own 18-foot-long trace.

We chose a plastic tandem kayak for the east coast, which offered speed, durability, volume, and—above all—safety.
Every other day John and I would switch positions to get a break from constantly looking at the back of each other's head and controlling the rudder.

Taking a short rest break to "stretch our legs" and look ahead for a possible route through the jammed-up ice.

This is different from the tandem formation, two-by-two, used where there are trees. My Inuit dogs are the same breed as those we planned to purchase in Greenland for the expedition. I would have loved to use my own expedition-experienced dogs on the trip, but the import of dogs to Greenland is forbidden due to the possible exposure of the native Greenlandic dogs to diseases for which they are typically not vaccinated.

* * * *

Our food for the trek consisted of about 1,800 pounds for the human team members and 7,500 pounds of specially formulated dog food. Our diet comprised foods that proved to be suitable on past arctic and antarctic expeditions and those used during my own past projects. We obtained most of it through natural foods cooperatives and then assembled breakfasts, lunches, and one-pot dinners to suit our nutritional requirements. We tested and used some new herbal products, MCT oils (medium chain triglycerides), and incorporated more easily digestible proteins such as nuts and beans. Oatmeal, pastas, rice, and potatoes were staples of the diet. Some unusual specialty items that were important to our high-calorie diet were honey candy, Halva (a Jewish sesame seed candy), pemmican (a mixture of dried pork, lard, and dried cranberries), powdered goat's milk, and dehydrated refried beans. These also provided a welcome change from the monotony of a strictly regimented and otherwise boring diet. A variety of foods boosts the morale, too.

For the dogs we began with a high-quality dog food used by dog mushers in Alaska and here in Minnesota. We then added a specially blended formula of fish oils and animal and vegetable fats for added calories in the extreme cold. The basic formula consisted of a 50-pound bag of dry dog food mixed with 7 pounds or 1 gallon of formula fat. Vitamin E was then added as a preservative. All this was mixed together and put in wax-coated fish boxes, making a 57-pound package. Funny how it ended up that each dog would be fed about the same amount as John and I would consume—2 pounds per day, or the equivalent of 5,600 calories. Hmmm . . .

Over fifty volunteers from the community assembled one Saturday and packed food from 10 a.m. to 11 p.m. With all the food laid out and arranged for packing, it hit home just how long we would be gone. I made a joke holding up two 55-pound sacks of oatmeal, saying, "When John and I finish this oatmeal, we can come home." Then I realized it was no joke!

Since we were working with different food components that, when combined, would provide the right mix of nutritional and caloric requirements, each meal had to be "assembled." All of the food was arranged into three assembly lines and volunteers began filling resealable plastic bags with the proper amount to make up a breakfast, lunch, or dinner for two. A breakfast, lunch, and dinner bag was then put into another bag and tied off to make one day of rations for two. The expedition plan called for a certain number of days of food to be placed at each of the thirteen depot locations around Greenland, so all the packaged food was organized into depots, packaged, labeled, and prepared for shipment.

Dog food mixing and packing went on until noon the next day. A cold, wet, sloppy morning found us scratching our heads and debating the best way to combine 110 gallons of warmed liquid fat with 5,000 pounds of dry dog food and package it in 24x30x8-inch wax-coated boxes. In the end we discovered that there wasn't any "good" way to do it. So we just opened each bag of dog food, poured in the fat, then boxed, taped, labeled, and hauled until it was done.

The kayaks and sledges were disassembled and wrapped in reinforced plastic for shipment. They looked like giant Tootsie Rolls as they lay next to the house waiting to be trucked to Minneapolis. Next, all of the boxed and labeled food was organized into depot locations and transferred to the largest U-Haul truck we could get for the five-hour drive. At our export shipper's main facility, we took over a large area of their warehouse so we could palletize the depots and organize them for shipment by boat to Greenland via Denmark and Iceland. The cargo that went to Iceland was then transferred to Station Nord in north Greenland by large aircraft. From there it was distributed by Twin Otter aircraft to eight extremely remote locations spaced 175 miles apart along Greenland's northern coastline.

Each of the thirteen supply depots contain 500 pounds of food, fuel, and gear, calculated to last the team for approximately fifteen days. To protect the food from bears and scavenging arctic fox in remote locations, the supplies were placed inside cages we fabricated using expanded metal grating held together at the corners by oval "quick links." These oval links allow the cages to hinge at the corners so they can be flattened and transported by airplane. Heavy rocks were added to the inside of the cages next to the food so bears couldn't drag the cage from its location.

Last-minute jobs consisted of mounting bindings on skis, sewing snow flaps on the tent, and putting together a repair kit of the essentials like Duct Tape, pliers, multi-screwdriver, extra cloth, spare parts for the stoves, and items for repairing kayak and dog sledge. We met with Dr. John Wood, a good friend and local physician, to review the contents of our medical kit. We discussed various scenarios regarding medical emergencies and what could happen on the expedition—appendicitis attack, broken bones, infections. The list could go on forever. With John's guidance and advice, we adjusted the kit according to the probability of each occurrence and whether we would be dog sledging or kayaking.

The main piece of survival clothing worn for kayaking is a one-piece dry suit with hood and is made of a waterproof, breathable material. This oversuit is outfitted with latex gaskets that seal off wrists and neck, and attached latex socks that keep the feet dry. In the event of capsizing into the frigid water, the suits would stave off hypothermia, keeping us alive for an hour or more—hopefully enough time for a self rescue. Thick neoprene-soled shoes are worn over the latex socks.

On sledging expeditions I use a combination of traditional Inuit clothing and modern-day synthetics. Most traditional fur clothing is extremely warm even when a person is inactive. But if you're moving a lot, such as skiing or pushing a sledge through rough ice, the clothing is too warm and restrictive. We often use layers of synthetic fleece with a nylon wind shell anorak and pants. This layering system allows us to regulate our body temperature by removing layers when skiing or running, and adding them when it is extremely cold or when we are stationary. During extreme cold we wear fur pants made from caribou or polar bear. Mittens are made from the leg fur of the caribou and there is always a wolverine fur ruff around the parka hood to protect your face from frostbite.

Finally, on May 12, 1997, we made the two-hour drive north from Grand Marais to Thunder Bay, Ontario, Canada. Most of the way I had a mix of thoughts that ranged from the awful awareness of leaving friends and family to "Have I forgotten anything?" At the airport, hugs, kisses, and best wishes followed John and me onto the aircraft. Our flight took us to Toronto, Ottawa, then up to Iqaluit, N.W.T., Canada, for the final leg to Kangerdlugssuaq, Greenland. From Kangerdlugssuaq we boarded a Dash 7 aircraft to Nussuaq in south Greenland and then got onto a Sikorski 61 helicopter to Paamiut, arriving on May 15.

I tried to make a journal entry every day, but there were times when we were just plain exhausted from the day's push and our eyes fell shut as soon as we went horizontal in the tent. Because of the length of the expedition, the days sometimes seemed to run into each other, making one seem much like the one before. I'm afraid we may have become somewhat numb to our surroundings. What now seems unbelievable or life threatening might hardly have evoked a comment from John or me.

The text and photos in this book can only touch on the endeavor as a whole, for Greenland is so vast, majestic, and complex that I can only hope to offer you a taste of our experience and what Greenland truly is.

Giving my skis a rest, I jumped on the sledge during pre-expedition training at Lake Nipigon, Ontario.

CHAPTER ONE

Kayaking the Unpredictable West Coast

May 15, 1997, Nuuk

It is one day before John and I are to depart on an expedition that has been two years in the making, and I am in fear and doubt for the first time. Many thoughts are running through my head: "Do we have all our ducks in a row? Or is this a suicide mission? Can our kayaks handle the long journey and seas ahead of us?" I'm sure John is having many of the same thoughts.

Somehow it's comforting to know that Kelly will remain behind in Nuuk when we chopper the 198 miles south to Paamiut to the official start. We will see her again when we arrive back here in two weeks' time.

May 16, 32°F, Paamiut—61°56′North 49°40′West

As John and I lashed our two polyethylene kayaks together in their catamaran configuration for today's departure, an elder Greenlandic man stopped by on his way to go hunting. He was scratching his head and wondering what we were up to. We told him that we were going to paddle to Qaanaaq, some 1,500 miles to the north. He just smiled, increasing the weathered wrinkles in his brown face, and said, "Good luck."

It was a still and sunny afternoon when we finally got underway. As we pushed off from shore, a cold breeze brought the smell of saltwater and seaweed. We wove our way around the unfamiliar pack ice using our paddles as push poles when necessary. It was a slow start. We made only 3 miles' progress in 3 hours.

Seals were plentiful around the aqua-blue sea ice and small clear pieces of icebergs. We now refer to these ice chunks as "bergy bits."

At Paamiut, the turquoise water means there is underlying ice that floated in from the Arctic Ocean. The long drift along the eastern coast of Greenland, waves, and the heat from the almost 24 hours of sunlight have sculpted the ice into many interesting shapes.

Seagull nests like this one are common among the thousands of small islands that skirt Greenland's coast. Eider ducks and terns are also abundant.

May 18

We are in an area of numerous small islands used by nesting waterfowl and seagulls. Although these islands break up the monotony and reduce the dangers of paddling in the open sea, they cause extra work in the navigation department.

The day started out calm, but a strong northwest headwind began at midday, our arms straining as we paddled against it. John and I tried to think of ways to make some progress into the wind.

We removed as much cargo as we could off the decks of our kayaks and stored what would fit under deck to cut down on wind drag. The further decision to reduce weight meant leaving some valuable gear and equipment on a small island with a gift-note to any Inuit egg gatherer who might find it. We also tried to "tack," using our sails for a zig-zagging strategy. But it didn't help. Our small sails were so inefficient at tacking that, in the end, we had to rely solely on paddles and muscle.

Troubled by the fact that we only made 5 miles today, John and I had long discussions about our options. Already, our arm and shoulder muscles are nearly wasted and to keep our strength up, we are consuming our limited food supply much faster than planned. We know it is impossible to paddle the remaining 1,487 miles if the wind keeps up like it is. We find ourselves remembering the words of the many people who told us this was impossible and questioning our plan. "Will we make it to the north before winter sets in?" "Have we made a mistake in our calculations?" "What were we doing out here anyway?"

It dawned on me today that, aside from its name, one of the greatest ironies about Greenland is that it is an island. It's so huge and vast that it overwhelms you. It should be called a continent. The other thing that is registering is just how isolated we are. There are no convenience stores just around the corner. There will be no phone call to Dad asking him to bring the car and pick us up.

All we can do is hope that the weather gets better as we go farther north and away from Greenland's turbulent southern waters.

Geography

Greenland, the world's largest island, lies northeast of the Canadian Arctic. More than two thirds of the massive body lies within the Arctic circle. Overall, Greenland is about 1,650 miles long and 750 miles across at its widest point—a landmass roughly fourteen times the size of England.

Its northernmost point, Cape Morris Jessup, is about 445 miles from the North Pole. The enormous Greenland ice cap covers approximately 85 percent of the land mass with a maximum thickness of 11,000 feet. Much of Greenland is ringed by mountains that confine the ice cap to the island's interior. Greenland's largest outlet glacier is the Humboldt Glacier, located in the extreme northwest, with a 60-mile face exposed to the sea. Almost 10 percent of the world's fresh water is locked in the ice cap. If it were to melt, it would raise the world's sea level 21 feet.

The coastline is heavily indented by fjords, which slice inland and offer the most habitable areas. These, historically, have been the location of almost all settlements. The largest present-day settlement is Greenland's capital, Nuuk, with a population of over 9,000. Greenland, however, still has no national network of roads or railways for land transport. Travel is by sea, air, or dog sledge.

Greenland's climate differs greatly between the coast and the interior. Temperatures along the southern coast range from an average of 18°F in January to a balmy 50°F in July. Comparable figures for the northwest coast are -15°F and 45°F. Inland and north coast temperatures range from a brisk February average of -53°F to a July average of 10°F.

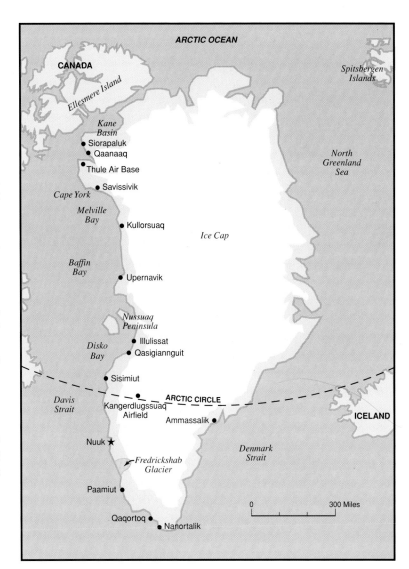

Kayaks

Our kayaks needed to be able to take the wear and tear of being dragged over rocks and the constant banging into ice. For this we chose and modified two 17-foot polyethylene kayaks so they could be catamaranned together for stability and so they could be sailed. A full-length kayak paddle was too long for stroking in the narrow center opening of the craft when it was in catamaran configuration, so we opted for break-apart, lightweight graphite kayak paddles and inserted a "T-handle" in one half, producing a short canoe paddle. The other halves of the paddles were stored under deck for spares or for reattachment, forming a double-blade kayak paddle when we wished to separate our kayaks and paddle them solo.

This picture was taken of us just prior to leaving Paamiut. This kayak configuration saved our lives on at least two occasions while making the numerous long sea crossings.

We outfitted our kayaks with two main sails and one spinnaker. Due to unfavorable winds, we were only able to use these for 165 miles of the 1,250 miles we kayaked on the west coast. On average, our paddle speed was 2 mph in the catamaran, 3 mph solo, and 6 mph sailing. We insulated the inside of our cockpits with closed-cell foam, to keep our legs warm against the cold conducted through the hull by the surrounding water.

For the east coast leg, we used a plastic, 19-foot, 26-inch-wide tandem kayak instead of two single kayaks. Each day John and I would switch positions, from front to back. The back person ran the foot controls for the kayak's rudder and the front guy would get a break from running the steering and looking at the back of a head for the day. Empty, the boat weighed 78 pounds. Loaded with two paddlers and 220 pounds of food and gear, it was brought to its maximum capacity.

Above: Just a little way out from camp, John dropped a fishing line on a cork. It will be retrieved in the morning with hopes of fish for tomorrow night's dinner.

Left: The mountains here, near Maniitsoq, were some of the most jagged we had seen on the whole expedition. We watched two fin whales pass by during the out-going tide as we ate our lunch.

Calm waters allowed us to paddle separately; we were hoping to increase our mileage. For many days, we had to navigate through the fog. It made us a bit nervous not knowing for sure what lay ahead, or if we would hit the little island we had marked on the map 9 miles away. To miss our objective after hours of paddling, could mean losing a day of travel retreating out of the many dead-end fjords.

May 19

Had a welcome break in the headwinds today and it couldn't have come at a better time. We had to travel for 15 miles in front of the notorious Fredrickshab Glacier, where the water is shallow. When the wind blows off the inland ice onto this glacier it can cause heavy wind and seas.

It was raining most of the day with periods of sun breaking through now and again. In the distance we saw the most amazing thing—a brightly colored rainbow touching down exactly on the picturesque summit of a massive berg. It made a beautiful and indelible impression on me, with the steel-blue water and dark rain clouds in the foreground. This is what it is all about for us. The rewards of hardship are starting to pay off.

May 20

We awoke at 3:00 a.m. to a crisp morning slightly above freezing. It was a foggy day with visibility less than 1/2 mile. For breakfast we managed to collect a few seagull eggs to supplement our rations. John, who is not big on eating eggs to begin with, kept calling them "fishy-tasting, boiled rubber balls," but ate them nonetheless.

The fog, thick as pea soup, forced us to rely on islands along our route, logged in as way points in our GPS (global positioning system). The fog magnified the apparent size of small pieces of ice, making us think it was a gigantic iceberg ahead, only to find out after a few feet that it was just a duck-size piece. This also held true for the small islands that seemed to pop out of nowhere. During these times of low visibility we have to be certain of our course to avoid traveling down some dead-end fjord.

We've started to find driftwood along the shore, deposited by melting polar pack ice. The driftwood comes from trees that fall into the rivers of Siberia and end up in the Arctic Ocean. To save on fuel we built a small three-stone fire for cooking and to dry wet gloves and boot liners.

May 21

Today, we came to our first of many long, open-sea crossings—5 miles. Our nervousness and feelings of vulnerability were compounded by a startling exhaling sound only yards from our kayak. We laughed away some tenseness when we realized it was a large minke whale surfacing for a dive.

As I did our usual radio check tonight with Nuuk, John was pulling in our dinner on a hook—a small polar cod he caught on a tiny piece of pepperoni used for bait. Nuuk informed us of more of the same weather to come—fog patches and stiff northwest winds. We are stronger now, but paddling into the wind and making much progress is still difficult.

May 24

It's still early in the season with temperatures around freezing during the day. At midday there was an expression of confusion on John's face, and I noticed a sluggishness when we got out of our kayaks for a break to relieve ourselves. At first I thought it was just fatigue from the days of hard paddling and reduced rations, but then became worried when his speech was also slurred. I realized it was the early stages of hypothermia. Too little food, damp clothing, and the heavy workload were the perfect recipe for it.

Hypothermia is a condition where the body's core temperature drops below normal. If left untreated it can become critical, resulting in coma and eventually death. Once hypothermia sets in, it becomes impossible to help oneself. When it happens to you, you never really recognize it. Fortunately, a partner who knows

Sitting on a trunk of driftwood, possibly from a thousand miles away, John warms himself next to a small fire—after his sobering bout of hypothermia.

the signs can almost always spot it.

I gave him some warm orange drink from our thermos and a prized chocolate bar, then dug out another sweater from the kayak for him. After a few hours he was back to his old self. But we still decided to call it quits for the day and camp.

May 26

Rose early to depart through choppy seas but only managed

½ mile before taking safe passage through a narrow gorge leading to a tidal estuary. Headwinds must be over 15 mph—makes paddling too difficult to continue today.

Outside the refuge of our tent, the weather turned into a two-day gale, allowing us plenty of time for rest and a much-needed body wash—something we have neglected lately. We both stood naked in an icy puddle of fresh water caught in the hollow of a flat rock. Rinsing my hair of soap was the worst, and the near-freezing water gave me an "ice cream" headache.

*But after the initial shock and a crisp wind
drying off our goosebumps, we agreed that the short bit
of torture was worth the clean feeling.*

We also took the opportunity to do some laundry and I was reminded of an interview I gave before leaving Minnesota. We were asked how often we changed undergarments. I replied, "Once a month—John changes with me and I change with him."

It got a good laugh at the time, but it certainly wasn't the truth. We try to wash our limited clothing during rest and storm days.

May 28

It was still a bit nasty and sleeting when we decided to leave this morning at 6:30 a.m. The VHF radio forecast called for a 24-hour lull in the storm before another gale would hit.

A handful of Ramen noodles and a skimpy little fish from which to make a broth-based soup was our total remaining food supply. We need to make Nuuk today—34 miles away. Our average mileage so far has been 13 miles per day. I wondered if we could do it.

The day started with a 15-mile crossing to a small island. During this 7-hour first leg we twice had to stand up in our kayak cockpits to urinate and stretch our sore backs and legs. We reached Nuuk at midnight after four brief rest stops and 17½ solid hours of paddling. Our numb arms and shoulders were beyond sore and aching—they were more like dead appendages, useless and without feeling. It was the hardest day in either of our memories. We would not be able to repeat it.

June 3, Nuuk

We needed the week in Nuuk to let our muscles repair and to lighten and modify our kayaks, anything to help give us an edge against the awful headwinds. We shaved 6 pounds of unneeded wood, plastic, and components off our kayaks with the help of a resident craftsman.

He told us that Nuuk is built on an exposure of the world's oldest known rock formation—3.86 billion years. He also informed us that spring is a month late this year. For some reason, we were not surprised.

It was great to see Kelly again in Nuuk. She's spending a month gathering information for the educational program. But our stay came all too quickly to an end, having to say goodbye until who-knows-when. Those goodbyes never get any easier.

Even though we were only able to sail 15 percent of the entire journey, it proved to be the most dangerous
mode of travel since the winds were only slightly favorable during the onset of a gale.

During our journey, we battled awful headwinds. They left us exhausted with aching, spent arms. Due to the direct headwinds, we resorted to pulling our kayaks along the coast with the bow line.

June 8

We've been kayaking Greenland's rugged west coast for the last three weeks, but nothing prepared us for what we experienced today. The weather and seas were as foul as we've ever seen them. The skies were dark with rain and the ocean a cold, unsympathetic blue-gray. The waters around us had been transformed into chaos by the onslaught of a sudden storm, and each successive mountain of water worked relentlessly to put an end to our efforts. Although our bodies are fit from days of paddling, we found it ever more difficult to keep from capsizing.

From the spray off the bow, I got a taste of seawater on my lips, constantly raw and chapped from the salt and 22 hours of sunlight. Our hands ached. They were numb with cold from water that penetrated through worn spots in our neoprene gloves. We knew that Greenland's weather was unpredictable—calm one minute and blowing a gale the next—but what began as an average day had rapidly deteriorated into a life-threatening open-water crossing, 5 miles from land.

We're fortunate that the kayaks were designed so they could be joined together catamaran-fashion and sailed during these long crossings. Attached side by side, barely 2 feet apart, they provided added stability, the only thing that kept us upright.

I sensed John's nervousness as he looked over his shoulder in anticipation of the next big wave. Busy with lines and steering, John shouted, "Here comes another one! Right rudder!"

We discovered that the combination of wind and ocean swell made every fifth wave the largest of a set. Bracing myself, I dropped my rudder to accompany John's, gaining better control of

June 5

Wanting to increase our speed by reducing weight, we decided to leave villages with only the bare minimum of food and to utilize the resources around us as we go. So sea urchins are now part of our diet. They can easily be scooped off the bottom of a shallow bay at low tide with a kayak paddle. Handling the spiny creatures with neoprene gloves, we split the hard shell with a knife. The slimy, orange-yellow contents are eaten raw, sliding down with a taste of soft butter. M-m-m-m!

the kayaks. We were running on a heading diagonal to our course—each wave fought to push us sideways, parallel to the wall of water. Caught in this storm and not wearing dry suits, we both knew the inevitable outcome if we were dumped into the frigid waters.

The wind increased and so did our speed, making a humming noise on the lines and sails. We soon found ourselves surfing out of control down the 8-foot waves, submerging the bow into the preceding wave. Water covered the deck and pressed in on our spray skirts.

Thoughts of Kelly and my son, Jacob, ran through my mind. I wanted to scream their names, but couldn't. Instead John and I yelled to each other over the wind and waves to reef-in our small main sails and relieve the spinnaker.

My sails were still partly up and blocked my view, so John shouted directions—right or left—to keep us on course. I plunged my paddle into the water, using it as a brake and to assist the rudders as we fought the sea to maintain our course for a tiny rock island. Seeking reassurance, I stole a glance at John's face. His look was one of shock combined with concentration as we stroked for the right side of the island. My face, I'm sure, reflected far worse.

Our objective was to get behind the island and make a landing; to our right, less than 50 yards away, a jagged rock shoal broke the surface, leaving little room for miscalculation. We steered for the area between the two, our single hope for safe passage. Everywhere else was being pounded by waves or it was too steep for a safe landing.

As we drew closer to the island, the wave heights increased

We were always uneasy about making long crossings between capes, even when the weather was good. It was more often than not that we would get caught in the middle and a storm would fight us every inch of the way to the shore and safety.

and the horizon was lost to immense walls of gunmetal-blue water. Sitting in a kayak, 6 inches below the waterline, we felt engulfed and overwhelmed by each successive wave. While in the trough of the wave, we saw nothing but water and a white froth at the top.

Then, as if by magic, the island was on our left side. We had to be careful not to run aground on the wave-pounded shoal to our immediate right. In less than 200 yards we would be safe, ducked protectively behind the island. But closing the gap

How nice it is to finally find a decent place to camp and rest. Exhausted, we begin looking for a spot to erect the tent.

between us and safety was achingly slow. Our muscles burned from the strain of constant exertion. Suddenly, the waves slackened around us, a near calm compared to what they had been just seconds before. Relief washed over us.

Cold, but somehow still sweating, we looked for a place to land. Our backs throbbed from the constant twisting and our legs, numb from several hours in the kayaks, wobbled as we dragged the kayaks high onto the rocks. The feeling of solid ground under my feet was wonderful!

For the first time in hours, John and I looked each other in the eye, simultaneously shaking our heads. Nothing needed to be said. We never want to go through that again.

We made 24 miles today. In total we have kayaked 250 miles and have 1,250 miles left to go before reaching our changeover point to dog sledge.

Reflecting on the bright side, I said to John, "Dog sledging this coming winter through polar night and with temperatures near 50 below looks pretty good right now."

Between strokes on the bilge pump, John flashed me an Aussie smile from behind his fast-growing red beard.

"Bloody right, mate," he laughed. "Bloody right!"

June 13

Today is a significant day for us. We went 26 miles in 11 hours, crossed the Arctic Circle, and crossed the mouth of the third largest fjord in the world.

In honor of the event, John and I were entertained by the sight and screeching sounds of Greenland white-tailed eagles that flew overhead. This rare bird is larger than the American bald eagle and is only found in Greenland's southwest. Fin and minke whales also showed themselves, revealed by their shiny black fins breaking the smooth water. They appeared near our shoreline camp, rhythmically coming in and out of the fjords with the tidal currents—like a wonderful aquatic dance.

Tonight I made a radio call to Nuuk, asking for a phone patch to our office in Minnesota. This is not often possible, but this time I got lucky and Gary Atwood answered the phone. I was able to relay news of our progress and information for use in the educational program. It was so good to hear a familiar voice!

Mussel shells garnish a piece of old whale vertebrae on the shore. Mussels are abundant in the protected back waters of most fjords. During low tide when the water drops several feet exposing rocky shoals, John and I would find mussels attached to a small piece of seaweed and gravel. It was hard work with cold fingers. As soon as we had two small bags of mussels, we had enough to make soup, or we would open them up with a knife and eat them raw. Slimy little devils!

Exploration

In the year 980, Erik the Red, exiled from his home in Iceland, ventured out across the northern seas in search of rumored lands to the west. Three years later he returned, with descriptions of a land that captivated his fellow Norsemen. For his second journey, between 500 and 700 Icelanders joined him, and eventually they departed in a fleet of 25 ships. With them went a huge cargo of cattle, horses, tools, household goods, and other necessities.

These people were drawn by stories of green pasturelands beside endless fjords of deep, blue water; by plentiful fishing and game; by endless, unoccupied lands that offered no boundaries to the far-ranging Norsemen. They were also drawn by a name—Greenland. In the judgment of Erik the Red, "Men would be ready to go thither if the land had a good name."

In the history of Arctic exploration, the immense island of Greenland sits as a tantalizing enigma, its massive ice cap second only to Antarctica in size. For years, explorers speculated on what lay inland, beyond the coastal mountains and the seemingly endless rim of ice and snow. Some even believed there existed a temperate interior, with green valleys and flowing, meltwater streams.

Throughout the second half of the nineteenth century, men and ships poked and surveyed the exposed coastlines and the fjords that slice inland from the sea. Some sought the Northwest Passage, others searched for those who had become lost, some struggled here and died, their ships locked in the crushing grip of polar pack ice. Even today, much of Greenland remains a mystery—immense, white, and silent.

The moon glows over a rounded, multi-year iceberg. Being stationary and grounded to the sea floor, icebergs such as this are exposed to the Arctic's brief summer melt.

Expedition Diet

Our food rations varied in calories and volume between the cold dog sledging campaign and the warmer kayaking journey. Primarily, more fat was consumed during the winter trip to stay warm. While kayaking, we ate more carbohydrates. In volume it was about 34 ounces per person, per day for winter sledging and 24 ounces for kayaking. However, we did periodically supplement our kayaking diet with berries, fish, mussels, and ducks as available from the land and sea around us.

We started the day with the expedition-standard oatmeal mixed with dried milk, brown sugar, and raisins followed by a multi-vitamin. We would wash down the "bloatmeal" with a cup of instant coffee. Other than the coffee, this was my least anticipated meal. John enjoyed it.

Lunch would be eaten throughout the day, divided between the two to four rest stops we would make. The main part of the lunch was either a sports energy/food bar or Skibskiks (a rock-hard boat cracker made in Denmark) and a grab bag of nuts and dried fruit. You could also pound a nail with these crackers or suck up several gallons of water from the bilges of the kayaks. Lunch also included a piece of pepperoni or dried fish. Soup or a hot fruit drink was available from a thermos, and for dessert a piece of chocolate or hard candy.

Our dinners were always looked forward to with ravenous eyes. The entrée varied and used as its main ingredient noodles, rice, dried potatoes, or refried beans and humus. This was mixed with a dried soup, powdered cheddar cheese, or some kind of dried tomato-based spice mix. To increase the fat content, we would add olive oil, peanut oil, or butter according to the day's workload or cold temperatures. During the dog sledging leg we would add 4 ounces of additional pemmican to the above. Halva, satisfied our sweet tooth, and hot cocoa finished off the meal.

Above: Deep in the warmer, protected fjords of central and south Greenland, we found an abundance of pea-sized blackberries, which grow low to the ground.

Right: We also found sea urchins. We either ate the yolk-colored contents raw, or cooked them with mussels to make chowder.

We were finally making some significant mileage north. It was the height of summer and the weather stabilized a bit, but we were concerned that an early advance of ice from the north could stop us.

June 14

Today we kept to our course by following inuksuks—small, ancient stone cairns on little islands and headlands. It required a sharp eye to see them, since they sometimes only consisted of one rock on top of another. Though few along the way, these primitive Inuit "road signs" were very helpful to John and me when we were in doubt of where we were.

The limited stimulation of the dull colors of gray rock, overcast skies, and snow has an effect on the mind. We are both glum

and a bit homesick. We topped the day off trying to find an elusive leak in John's kayak that is getting our food wet. We are not the only things taking abuse on this trip.

June 20, Sisimiut ("people at the foxholes")

I was very happy to be closing in on the village of Sisimiut and the sound of howling dogs—music to my ears. This is the southernmost village in Greenland with sledge dogs and I am reminded that dog sledging is my first love—kayaking a distant second, especially after today's wild ride in an unexpected gale.

The sea was like glass one minute and the next we were at half sail, moving at 7 knots in 4-foot seas. Caught in a sudden gale, we searched the shoreline for a suitable place to beach our kayak. There was none. Beyond the bend, the coast ahead looked no better. We decided to attempt a landing on a 7-foot section of gravel between a sheer cliff and a mound of rock rubble. Remaining stationary by back-and-forth paddling just outside the breaking surf, we tried to time our landing using the largest wave of the set to drive us far up onto the shore, hoping this would give us time to get out and move the kayaks farther up the beach before the next wave hit.

But our timing was off, and we were still in the boats when the next wave hit. It threw us up onto the rocks, gouging a chunk of plastic out of our bow. As the wave receded, we were carried out with it in time to have the next breaking wave slam us against the sheer cliff, bending and disabling our rudder.

Real fear gripped me when I saw that one of the lashings that held the kayaks together had snapped. I knew we had to get off the rocks before the next wave swamped us and crippled the boats entirely. Seconds seemed like forever. Only frantic paddling fueled by terror and adrenaline got us clear.

Shakily, we paddled another mile down the coast and attempted a similar, hair-raising landing. This time Mother Nature smiled on us. I was thankful we hadn't elected to use lighter, more fragile, composite kayaks. At this point, John wryly reminded me of an earlier promise to ourselves. "So, we said we were never going to let ourselves get caught in one of those storms again, huh?"

This was the second time on the expedition I have been absolutely scared to death!

June 21–22

It's the longest day of the year, with the sun not setting below the horizon for the full 24 hours. And it is Greenland's National Holiday. Throughout the country, there will be drum dances, outdoor cooking, and games. Everyone looks forward to the short, but sweet, summer because it gives relief from the harsh, dark winter.

June 30

We slept well and woke late in the morning to hundreds of screaming arctic terns circling above our tent. We had inadvertently set camp near their nests. As we exited the tent and moved about, they would dive-bomb us with lightning speed and then resume their hovering position 100 feet overhead. It reminded me of a certain Alfred Hitchcock film. I am amazed that this agile bird has any energy left after its 20,000 mile yearly migration

Taking advantage of the midday sun, John and I take a well-needed rest. I caught up on my journal entries and John repaired his spray skirt with silicone and duct tape.

between the Arctic and Antarctic regions.

We left camp expecting the good, calm conditions of Disko Bay and feeling quite nervous. We had two extremely long kayak crossings of around 11 miles each, with a small island in the middle, to reach its eastern shore. We left in calm conditions, but after about an hour, the wind increased from the north to about 13 mph. The sea became very choppy, making the paddling more difficult, and we took cold water into the cockpit from around our spray skirts.

Looking like lead crystal, sun-cupped ice from clear, fresh glacial water frozen during past winters, now floats free, melting in the warmer sea.

about the next crossing. The conditions were "iffy" and the margin of safety not the best, but I couldn't go through the paddle grind we had experienced earlier in the day. The wind was right and I wanted to sail. If we were to go, it had to be now while the wind was in our favor and before it got too strong. I stressed my points, but knew it was dangerous and had to let John make his own decision to go or not. John firmly replied, "Yes, the wind will be at our backs and the waves don't look bad from here. But what will the waves have built to when we get across the fjord? They'll definitely be bigger!"

Feeling pressured by me he said yes. We donned our dry suits for a crossing that seemed to never end. Two-thirds of the way across, 7-foot swells pounded the small of our backs. Nervous and frightened, I apologized then and there for the pressuring. But we were lucky. Three hours later we entered Qasigiannguit. It was 1:30 in the morning. Limp with fatigue, we erected our tent on the beach and collapsed into it, too tired to climb the hill to the village.

We quickly became annoyed at the discomfort of sitting in ice water from the waist down, as we hadn't bothered to wear our dry suits. There was no place to pull up and sponge out the water. If we were to stop, we would take even more slop onboard by removing our spray skirts and also be pushed back by the swell. Exhausted, we pushed through the wind and waves until we found a suitable stopping place on the island to dry off and sleep.

Around three hours later we awoke pasty-eyed to a brisk west wind. And for the first time on the expedition John and I disagreed

July 3, Illulissat

Our final leg to Illulissat took us across the mouth of the dangerous Illulissat ice fjord. On local advice, we opted to go offshore, detouring five miles around the large bergs. We tried to keep a safe distance in case one calved a house-size piece crushing us. You could hear them thunder as they groaned and rubbed against each other. Trying to shave strokes off our detour, we ended up between several bergs—all the while praying they would give us the right-of-way.

We were sometimes startled, jumping in our seats at the sound of a large piece breaking off and plunging into the sea. By the time we reached the opposite side of the fjord, we had gained a lot more respect for the dangers these giants pose.

July 10

Today we made our longest open-water crossing thus far—19 miles. Then, tired as we were, we hauled our kayaks about 60 feet above the waterline. This was to prevent huge waves created by a calving iceberg from destroying our kayaks or washing them away. Inuit hunters have died this way, marooned on an island to die of thirst and hunger, and we didn't want to join them.

The many icebergs in the area have us pinned to shore. Even though the water may be hundreds of feet deep, the huge bergs still run aground before reaching the rock face of the shoreline, and allow only a narrow waterway through which we can proceed.

With almost 24 hours of light, we often switched our paddling to nighttime—between 11 p.m. and 10 a.m., when the sea is much more stable.

July 14, Nussuaq "big peninsula"
70°49′ North 54°12′ West

Even small delays count up and are depleting our food supply ahead of schedule, so we are cutting back on daily rations, becoming thinner and weaker each day. John is trying his hand at fishing again and managed to catch a small flounder. It was barely big enough to feed a house cat, but nevertheless a welcome addition to our depleted diet.

Paddling has been impossible due to strong headwinds, so for four days we have pulled the kayaks on a line, walking the rough shoreline in our awkward rubber boots. Progress is very slow. The kayaks get caught in the ice and rocks near shore, so we take turns dislodging them with a piece of driftwood as we creep along.

July 16

Both John and I are fatigued from paddling and tired of the wet and foggy days. I was at an all-time low today, physically and mentally drained from the recent difficult days.

In the past, when loneliness or homesickness began creeping in, I'd just erase it from my mind and try not to think about it—

At times, we felt very much alone, the moon aloft in the empty sky with only our tent for security and comfort.

remove the concept from my database, so to speak. But lately this hasn't been working. I was worried about myself—questioning my abilities and thinking that others were right—this is a stupid, impossible thing to do.

But today I had an experience that changed all of that.

We heard an unusual squawk from the nearby hill while we were making camp. At first we ignored it as we thought it would soon quit. While John finished setting up the tent, I decided to climb up the hill where I could get better reception for a scheduled radio call with Kelly. As I began my ascent, the squawk became louder, as if it were calling me to a certain location. I still couldn't make out where or what type of bird was making this unusual noise. It wasn't until I had peered over the summit that I saw, standing on a large rock near the peak, a raven.

Having heard many calls from ravens in the past, I immediately thought to myself that this call was slightly strange. The bird appeared to be carrying something with its right claw. But whatever it was, he was not really carrying it. It was attached to his leg and because of that he was making short 3- to 4-yard flights from rock to rock and landing hard on his feet.

I was curious to get a closer look at what was on his leg.

For some reason I sensed that he was trying to get my attention—bending over when he squawked, with wings flared, not seeming to mind me getting closer. I knew he could fly and was surprised at how close he was allowing me to come.

I was able to make out a small piece of driftwood—an inch in diameter and a foot long—caught in a woolly substance that was wrapped around his leg.

There was a special aura that seemed to develop around the situation—one that gave me a sense of spiritual uplift. It was something I desperately needed.

Through all of my involvement in the Arctic and my association with the indigenous cultures of the north, I have learned that they all have one particular thing in common: the raven is both a spiritual and sacred reincarnation of a great hunter or shaman.

I started to talk to the bird in an effort to get closer, and had the strange feeling that with tilts of his head, we were somehow communicating that we both had a problem and maybe we could help each other out—me with my efforts to cope with the demands of the expedition and being away from home, and he with this darn thing stuck to his leg that he couldn't get off.

Leaning against the same rock that the bird was perched on, I spoke to him in a low, convincing voice of help. I asked him if he would allow me to remove the debris from his leg, thus saving his life, and then asked if he could give me the strength and safe passage we needed for the expedition. As I came closer with arm and hand outstretched, I could see the fine features of his shiny black feathers and broad wedged beak. As I saw the details in his eyes, as if he were looking directly into mine, he picked up a small rock the size of a pea, holding it in his beak, displaying it to me as if to say, "This is all I have to offer you for your help." I suddenly felt bad asking him for something in return for saving his life.

It was always a bit intimidating to head into the fog and the unknown, with only our compass to guide us.

Closer, I carefully grabbed him by the legs so as not to hurt him in his second thoughts of escape. I noticed the material that was keeping the stick bound to his leg was muskox wool, a resource that most birds in the Arctic use for nesting purposes. In his nest-building efforts, he had managed to tightly secure the driftwood to his leg by this durable material and it caused him some pain. He pecked me as I worked to remove it. Finally he was freed, none the worse for wear. I tucked in his wings, and let go of him in a mid-air upswing with my arms. Expecting him to fly a long way from his capture, I was delighted that he only flew to a

large rock a few yards away, and looked back at me. He squawked as if to say, "Thank you," and then flew off over the mountain.

Smiling with renewed energy, I looked down at John in the valley doing the same old camp chores we have been doing for the past two months, completely unaware of what had just happened and its impact on me. I then turned my eyes onto the horizon and felt a growing eagerness to continue our expedition.

July 17

We are getting cold more frequently due to the reduced rations and hard work. Even John's toes are getting cold, leading him to remark that "they feel like wood." I knew that this was also caused by lack of circulation in our lower bodies during the 14 hours of twisting in the seats of our cockpits.

The steep coastline did not allow us to beach and rest—the long day had us cold, exhausted, and hungry. Stiff with fatigue, we finally found a sandbar created by the outflow from a small river and decided to camp. We climbed out of our kayaks bent over like two old men.

With food on our minds we were glad to spot mushrooms. We had been told that all mushrooms found growing wild in Greenland are edible—and this seemed like a good time to find out!

July 24

The sun made a rare appearance through the fog, warming the tent by late morning.

It's starting to get colder now as we proceed north, sighting more pockets of snow on hillsides. Frost and grease ice (a thin frozen film that forms on seawater) are present during early morning. We plan to take on more food and fuel to combat the colder temperatures that we expect north of Upernavik. We hope to change our fuel from kerosene to something cleaner burning for our stove. Everything is covered with the smelly soot of this stuff and the food even tastes of it.

It was too windy to make the 4-mile crossing today, so we camped near an essential source of fresh water provided by a melting sheet of snow on the hillside. We spent the down time reassessing the schedule required to finish in Qaanaaq before winter hits. We figured that we would need to average 21 miles each day in order to reach our goal before bad weather pins us down around September 1. This is taking into account essential rest and bad weather stops. Our average so far on the trip has only been 16 miles per day. This may be a tall order to fill, but we have to try.

What we need are more of those rare days of glass-flat water when one only has to move his arms and daydream to make good progress. One such day, out of sheer boredom, I counted 1,800 strokes of my paddle to cover a mile, keeping rhythm with the crinkling sound of my salt-stiff clothing.

August 3, Upernavik

What has been a constant fear of John's and mine during the whole journey happened today. We were paddling in the kayaks as separate craft when a house-size piece of ice suddenly exploded off an iceberg just to our left. John was a few yards ahead of me and I yelled, "Damn! Watch out for the wave!"

Reacting quickly to the wall of water, we each maneuvered our kayak to point into the wave. Fear propelled us as we rode the wave up high using our paddles to help stabilize ourselves. Rows

It was great to be heading north into the midnight sun on a stable sea—the downside was the quickly dropping temperatures of nighttime travel.

of progressively smaller waves followed, and we felt relieved that we had been able to avoid a life-threatening dip in the freezing water.

But our relief was short lived as the scenario worsened. When the waves rammed an iceberg to our immediate right, they made a car-size piece explode off right before our eyes. Caught between the two bergs we were fighting the crisscrossing waves.

The seriousness was evident on our faces for we knew what would happen if we both went into the water—our bodies would be robbed of heat in seconds.

After 17 hours of paddling, we were exhausted. There were only cliffs with no place to get out of the boats. With no place flat enough for a sleeping bag or tent, we slept fully clothed, sitting up. Our rest was uneasy as we thought about loose rocks falling from above.

Then a domino effect seemed to go on forever: the vibrations from each calving sending percussions through the berg, breaking huge pieces off the opposite side. Then another, and another. The warehouse-size bergs became topsy-turvy, rocking back and forth in slow but immensely powerful motions.

And here we were, sitting in two kayaks on an otherwise beautiful day, fighting for our lives, avoiding splash after splash. After ten minutes, all was calm and still again as if nothing had happened. I shiver when I imagine how it might have ended.

August 4

In the morning we awoke to find that the high-tide mark from the sea came within 8 inches of our tent. We were so tired we hadn't even heard the waves breaking so near our heads!

Later in the day we had to negotiate lots of glacial ice and bergy bits tightly jammed into a narrow passage between their parent bergs. Following the coast we approached the exposed cape with swells rising to 7 feet. The wind had been light, but gusts started getting stronger. There was little shelter on the northern, windward shore, so we were committed to rounding the peninsula's cape to find shelter.

The point was rough. Large waves loomed behind us and crashed over our decks. Backwash had surged out from the cliff and had jacked up the approaching swells. Waves also hit nearby icebergs, sending spray skyward. The tops of the waves were being blown off and spray was thick, stinging our eyes.

Rounding the point, we sped along rapidly. By this time it was blowing at least 40 mph. Finding a pebbly beach, we braced

It was not always easy to find a place to perch our tent during a storm or on the steep coastline.

ourselves for a surfing landing. I released my spray skirt and leapt onto the forward deck as we were driven up the shore, pushed by a huge wave. We tugged and hauled the boats up the shore, safely away from the menacing surf.

But while we were erecting the dome tent, a gust hit and broke two poles. A quick fix was aluminum ferrules and duct tape, carried just for this emergency. Once the tent was up, we placed large boulders all around on the tent's snow flap and tied everything down. It had turned into quite a storm, not really expected for early August.

Bloodlines

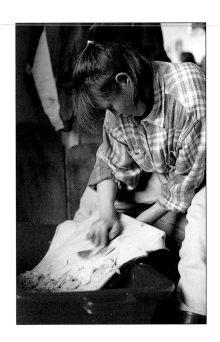

The vast majority of the inhabitants of Greenland are Greenlanders, a mixture of Inuit (Eskimo) and Scandinavian immigrants, primarily from Denmark. Some isolated traditional villages of pure Inuit can still be found in the extreme northwest. All the Inuit people are believed to be of Mongolian descent.

In the mid 1800s, the Thule Inuit were in fear of extinction. Only small groups remained around the Cape York and Etah areas. There were two main reasons for this decline in population: forgotten hunting techniques and a stressed gene pool. Certain hunting techniques had been lost with many of the elders who had died quickly and in large numbers from disease and famine.

Because of their extreme isolation, the Thule Inuit had no new genetic influence. The vast and uninhabited Melville Bay was to the south, the Kennedy Channel and the North Pole to the north, to the west was the ocean, and to the east was the ice cap.

In 1862 an Inuit shaman named Qitdlarssuaq and a group of his followers arrived in northwest Greenland in search of Inuit people and a better place to live. They had traveled on foot and by dog sledge on a three-year journey from Canada's Baffin Island.

They met the people of the Thule area and reintroduced the kayak, bow, and fish spear. These new implements brought more food variety to the villages. They provided fish and caribou to the diet. Because of the kayak, more marine mammals like walrus, seal, and narwhal could be hunted.

Qitdlarssuaq and his party intermarried with their fellow Inuit, providing new blood. Life was better after Qitdlarssuaq and his followers joined the Polar Inuit. Shortly thereafter, the introduction of rifles and traps from the early polar explorers made hunting even easier, helping the population continue to increase.

Above: After the meat is removed, the fat is scraped from the seal skin with an ulu. The hide will be stretched for use in making kamiks.

Left: The village of Savissivik, looking north toward Cape York. At the top of Cape York stands a tall cairn in memory of American polar explorer Robert E. Peary. It can be seen with binoculars from the village.

Polar Bears

Most all bears are hunted by dog team, but there are some instances where a hunter in a boat may spot them swimming between ice floes.

Polar bear hunters in the Qaanaaq district travel to the far north of Kane Basin or south to Cape York to hunt bears, and they can be gone for a month or more. From every kill, the meat is eaten and the skins are used to make the prized nanus (polar bear pants) that the hunters wear. They are durable and extremely warm. A big bear will provide three pairs of nanus.

To find a polar bear, the dog team and hunter will travel until they come upon a set of tracks fresh enough to leave a scent that the dogs can follow. Finally, it is spotted, and the dogs run in full pursuit of the bear. The hunter releases two or three of the dogs from the sledge so they can catch the bear, while the others follow behind. As the hunter gets closer, he will cut the remaining dogs loose to hold the bear at bay until he arrives and shoots it.

Before they had rifles, the hunters would spear the bear which was very dangerous. Many men and dogs have lost their lives in pursuit of this large carnivore, but the prized meat and skins make the challenge worth the risk.

A young man from Kullorsuaq out hunting seals shot this small polar bear running and swimming between ice flows. This will provide him nanus, or polar bear pants (left), for the cold winters.

51

The closer we came to Kullorsuaq, the more often we had to push off the floating ice bits with our paddles, zig-zagging the last few miles.

The wind eased enough to allow us to gather water and cook a meal. But the respite was short-lived. We soon had to yell at the top of our lungs to communicate. Our wet clothing hung in the apex of the tent, swinging back and forth.

At one point, we heard a loud crack and discovered that a guy rope had pulled its eyelet through the tent fabric. We slept with earplugs, but this only helped slightly. We spent the next eighteen hours in our sleeping bags, much of them awake and listening to the sound of 75 mph winds outside.

August 7

After a 17-hour day of paddling, we are still short of reaching the village of Kullorsuaq ("the devil's thumb") by 6½ miles. We were unable to stop and make camp sooner because of the sheer rock face of the coastline. We opted to perch ourselves on a barren strip of steeply inclined shore composed of scattered boulders. At 11 p.m., we pulled the kayaks up the ledge, anchoring them to a crack in the rock. For the next five hours, we practically slept in the kayaks. We remained fully clothed, leaning against the rocks for lack of a flat place to lie down.

August 8, Kullorsuaq

As we approached the village through an iceberg-cluttered channel, we encountered three small boats of hunting families heading off to their favored areas. They must have radioed ashore because, as we landed on the small dock, a crowd of around fifty men, women, and children gathered to meet us. We heard a rifle sound off five shots and a large round of applause was given as we stepped ashore. We were very pleased by the reception, though slightly shy and embarrassed by all the attention. The assembled crowd was quite amazed to learn that we had paddled all the way from Paamiut—1,250 miles away. This was the longest recorded kayak journey in Greenland. "Not bad," I thought, "since Greenland is home to the kayak."

August 9

In Kullorsuaq, there is a village bath house and one nurse, and all water is carried by the residents to their homes, usually in wheelbarrows. The small houses and huts are heated by little fuel oil

Kayaks like this one in Kullorsuaq are still used in northern Greenland for hunting narwhal and sometimes walrus. There is a self-imposed regulation that narwhals can only be hunted from kayaks or with dog teams from the ice edge. No motor boats or snow-machines are allowed in the hunt. This rule is to ensure a strong population of narwhals and keep alive the culture of kayaking and kayak building. In the recent past, kayaks were made of high-maintenance seal skin as a covering, but today most use cotton canvas and linseed oil.

Seal skin is widely used by the Greenlanders to make durable and waterproof mittens, jackets, pants, and footwear. Most jackets and pants are made with the fur left on, whereas most boots and mittens are made with the hairless and sun-bleached seal skin.

heaters. It is here we met Nikolai Jensen, a locally famous hunter who is held in high esteem. This kind old gentlemen no longer goes on long hunting trips, but possesses a great knowledge of the region and its character. He is sometimes referred to as "The Compass of Melville Bay," alluding to his having survived fifty trips by dog sledge, kayak, and boat to the village of Savissivik, 189 miles to the north.

During our time here, both Nikolai and John had birthdays. All the village folk were invited to a kaffemik, a casual gathering and invitation for all to stop by to share in coffee, tea, local fare, and sweets. Nikolai and John exchanged gifts. John received a traditional Greenlandic drill made from wood, bone, and sinew. Needless to say, John was quite honored in accepting this creation. John gave Nikolai a gold and enameled Emperor penguin stickpin, a symbol of his association with another of the world's ice caps, Antarctica.

As we left the celebration, the sledge dogs were howling in chorus and a newly fallen snow covered the hills. We could see a group of hunters returning in their small boats. Their hunting foray had produced four narwhal and a nanoq (polar bear). All were smiling and happy that they had procured this good supply of food for the harsh winter ahead.

August 14

Today, we learned that this would be the end of our kayak travel for this season. The daily satellite reconnaissance maps of the Melville Bay region showed hazardous pack ice blocking the way north to Savissivik. Local hunters confirmed this. The only areas of open water were 15 to 20 miles out to sea, with no chance of taking refuge on land should a storm come up. If we were to travel the area at this time, two possible fates could befall us—we could be crushed by wind-driven sheets of pack ice, or an offshore gale could push us out into the seas of Baffin Bay. Even the large coastal trading ship had been unable to reach the isolated village of Kullorsuaq due to the ice.

The decision was made to continue north to the Qaanaaq district by umiatsiaq, a small open boat used for hunting and fishing, and attempt to reach the district's small village of Savissivik and then on to Thule Air Base. (Our kayaks will be cargoed on the trading ship to south Greenland, and then back home via Denmark.) The umiatsiaq, though still risky, can break through thin ice and push its way through small pans of ice blocking the path, where kayaks cannot. The craft's maneuverability also allows it to dodge crushing ice floes. Our difficult job now was to find someone willing to go with us on this hazardous journey.

Near Nikolai Jensen's house, the dog sledges are elevated, away from ground moisture and chewing dogs. The washing machine and generator on the front porch came from Denmark.

August 21

After three different hunters refused to travel to Savissivik in the Qaanaaq district because of the dangers, Martin Olsen and his father Gabriel, both competent hunters and umiatsiaq drivers, agreed to take us.

We left around noon and promptly encountered a returning group of local hunters. Learning where we were headed, they were happy to provide a small supply of freshly caught narwhal mattak (skin). The highly nutritious skin and the layer of attached blubber are cut into small pieces and chewed, yielding a pleasant nutty flavor. The oily snack would help increase our caloric consumption, helping us stay warm during the cold journey ahead.

The farther north we went, the more congested the pack ice became. Using binoculars we tried to pick a path through the ice fields. The ice near Savissivik was almost solid pack. We tried many times to find a passage around a nearby island and each time met with impassable ice. From the bow we used large poles to try to push the pans away as Martin skillfully used his motor to

A hunter from Kullorsuaq heads south through a narrow opening between an iceberg and land. He is hunting for seals.
The supply ship that comes here each year has been unable to arrive yet due to heavy ice.

make headway. Backing up after becoming wedged between two large pieces, we were thrown off balance by the boat's abrupt stop. We had rammed into a large ice pan lying submerged just below the surface. Martin tipped the motor forward to examine the damage and John and I stared at it in shock. Three blades of the propeller had snapped off. We suddenly felt like lame ducks, at the mercy of the menacing ice pack that waited to crush a hole in the hull of our fragile boat.

Martin, however, was unperturbed. He reached under his seat and produced a beat-up spare prop, on hand for just such an occasion. He made a quick switch and we were able to persevere, pushing and prodding from the bow, turning and pushing with the motor. Hours ticked by and we were no closer. Then it started to snow, and a south wind sprang up. The wind could set the pack ice moving, and this could prove disastrous if we got caught between moving floes.

We managed to anchor to the rocky point and, being slightly in the lee of the wind and current, stayed afloat in a patch of open water no bigger than a small swimming pool. We stayed put for about 7 hours, sleeping on the cold floor of the boat. On awakening, a survey of the ice conditions showed little improvement. About 16 hours later and running short of gas, we finally found some open water and made our way into the village. We were all very tired and welcomed the hot meal of freshly caught seal washed down with piping-hot mugs of coffee.

We spent the next few days recuperating and visiting in Savissivik, which means "the place of knives or steel." It was

John is measuring the wind speed during a lull in a storm. A few hours earlier the wind peaked at 75 mph, wreaking havoc on our tent. The storm left large blocks of ice on the shore from the pounded icebergs at sea.

Netting appats in Savissivik. Each year, the village nets around 50,000 of these little birds to be eaten either raw as they are caught, boiled, or made into Kiviaq. During early winter the sealskin and birds are retrieved and eaten. Appats are a main part of the Polar Inuit diet.

named for the meteorites that have been found there. At some time in the past, the Inuit recognized the value of these extraterrestrial visitors and began chipping off pieces of the meteorites to make knives and harpoon heads.

The village of around eighty people is located at the base of a rocky escarpment that is inhabited in the summer by hundreds of thousands of appaliarsuk, small awk-like birds. The tons of excrement deposited over the years have produced a large mossy shore on which the village is situated.

The village depends on these birds for survival, capturing them in hand-held, hooped nets as they fly by. The birds are eaten fresh or eaten as kiviaq—fermented for six months in sealskin, feathers and all. When the sealskin is opened, the smell and taste is similar to that of blue cheese.

After five days, it was time to say farewell to our generous hosts, and move on to our winter destination of Qaanaaq, home of the Polar Inuit. We feel a great sense of accomplishment and have already seen more Greenland coastline then most Greenlanders. We are able to give an overall view of what Greenland is like and its culture. To have done it a stroke at a time, I can say we were thorough.

August 22, Qaanaaq—72°27′ North 70°40′ West

The village of Qaanaaq is located at the mouth of a large fjord that provides good hunting. The town of around 600 people is the home of the Avanersuaq community. This Greenlandic name means "the northernmost place," but actually, a small village

58

named Siorapaluk is located a little farther north and is truly the most northern village in the world.

August 23

A blizzard today, and the weather has deteriorated rapidly since the last of the midnight sun. The temperatures are starting their descent, averaging around 27°F, and we have had almost continuous snow and storms.

Today I came across Jens Danielsen, an Inuit I first met a few years back on a previous expedition. He had just returned from an unsuccessful narwhal hunt down the fjord. He looked toward the southern skies saying, "Naamannqitsoq" (bad). Another major storm is brewing and is disheartening news to the hunters who have not been able to successfully hunt because of the weather. "We need fresh meat and our dogs are hungry as well. Winter has come too soon this year."

Later that evening the storm reached record wind speeds of 180 mph at Thule Air Base, just to our south, the second strongest winds ever recorded here. Even though John and I had hoped to kayak the last 270 miles from Kullorsuaq to Qaanaaq the umiatsiaq journey was plenty for us. We feel very fortunate that we are not kayaking and bobbing around in Melville Bay right now! A storm of that magnitude would surely have put an end to us had we been there.

During a storm, the dogs curl up in a ball to conserve energy, allowing the snow to blow over them, encasing them in their own "igloo."

The Tip of the Iceberg

A dark piece of seaweed absorbs heat from the sun, which has melted into the glacial ice.

An iceberg can be defined simply as a large mass of floating ice. But when you are in a kayak and encounter one, this definition seems woefully inadequate.

In the Northern Hemisphere icebergs are of glacial origin and usually have picturesque shapes, frequently pinnacled or domed. Arctic icebergs, for the most part, are products of Greenland's ice cap. The pressure exerted by the massive ice cap produces rivers of ice, or glaciers, that forge their way slowly through coastal mountains and into the fjords. As the glacier edge moves into the sea, the combination of tidal action and the buoyant forces of the water break off pieces of the protruding ice. The broken-off pieces become icebergs. The process of breaking off is called "calving." Of the 20,000 icebergs calved from Arctic glaciers, most originate from about twenty active glaciers located on the west coast of Greenland between 68 degrees and 78 degrees north latitude. The bergs are carried northward and westward by the West Greenland current, until eventually many of them are caught up in the southwesterly moving Baffin Land and Labrador currents.

Ordinarily, the largest bergs observed in Arctic regions are 400 to 500 feet long and about 250 feet above sea level. Only about one eighth of the mass of an iceberg is above the water. The ratio of an iceberg's vertical height above water to its height below water may vary considerably because of the irregular shape of bergs. Usually, the above-water height is about one fourth to one third of the maximum below-water height.

When traveling near large icebergs, we typically tried to give them a wide berth. Even at a distance of 500 to 750 feet, we could still look down below our kayaks and see the berg below us, disappearing into the depths. A real danger was the ever-present possibility of being hit from below or swamped by a large berg piece breaking off beneath us and exploding to the surface like a cork. The only warning is a boiling turbulence just before the piece breaks the surface.

This undermining makes the bergs dangerously unstable and top heavy as ice chunks dislodge below the waterline or melt away with time. Even though most roll-overs generally happen in slow motion, we could still get flattened by one, and the shifting of the berg's weight can cause further calving. Even when no calving occurred, there were many instances when the surrounding sea ice blocked a fast getaway from the rolling berg's path and we seemed to be chased by a huge, tipping piece of ice.

The stormy sky around this mammoth berg creates an eery silhouette, silent but dangerous.

CHAPTER TWO

Dog Sledging in the North

With the conclusion of the west coast kayak portion of the expedition, we were confronted with a 5½-month training period in the Qaanaaq region during Greenland's polar night. While refining our traveling techniques and working with our newly acquired dogs, we would also be relaying cultural information to our educational program in the United States.

At the end of polar night in February, with sledges loaded, we will be heading north with only our huskies, the cold, and the newly risen sun for company.

Hearing that we would need dogs, Mamarut Kristiansen had brought two very wild dogs by boat from Qeqertarssuaq (Herbert Island). They were so big and so skittish that John and I wondered how he even got them in the boat to begin with. It was apparent that as pups, these two had never become accustomed to people. They had probably run free on the island, scavenging what they could for food. Equal in size at about 100 pounds, both had massive box-shaped heads and bent ears, giving the appearance of furry, four-legged tanks. We named the beige-colored one Tyson after he tried to bite off John's ear while John was trying to get a harness on him. The white-and-black one naturally became Holyfield. It was apparent that not even Mamarut—a man with a reputation as a great sledge dog driver—had the desire to tame them. Or maybe he was just looking forward to the fun of watching us try it.

On the bright side, these two brothers were big, strong, and at the prime age for expedition work.

A rare "sun dog," created—for just a moment—by airborne ice crystals reflecting the sunlight.

Sponsorship and educational project commitments, further logistical arrangements, and the need to deal with our still precarious funding status, necessitated my return to the United States for part of this period. John remained in Qaanaaq, assembling dogs for our two teams, training them to work together as one, and finalizing placement of critical, intermittent supply depots in Siorapaluk and Rensselaer Bay, 100 miles to the north. He was also able to get to know the people of Qaanaaq and the surrounding villages in a way that would have otherwise been impossible.

Plus, after nine months of pre-expedition work and the last three months spent together in the kayaks, it gave us a much-needed break from each other.

Fall Freeze-up and Polar Night

The sun disappeared below the horizon in Qaanaaq, setting on October 26, giving way to four months of polar night, and will not rise again until February 17.

Titsarfik (November) also means "one is listening," and is the month of waiting in Greenland. The 1,000 or so dogs in the Qaanaaq district are especially excited with the newly fallen snows, sensing that a new sledging season is upon them. The sea ice will soon be frozen thick enough to travel on, but both people and dogs must wait patiently and "listen" for the sounds of winter's advancement and the sea ice slowly freezing.

Polar night is a time of striking beauty during the full moon. The light cast by the moon and stars reflects brightly off the snow and ice, sometimes providing enough light to read. When the moon takes the place of the sun in these latitudes it creates a world of its own, a world of mysterious grays and shadows. On the darkest day of the year, December 21, it's so dark you can't see a thing, day or night. Greenlanders keep themselves entertained by visiting each other's homes, chatting over tea, and playing games. As the months of darkness and melancholy linger on, the people grow more eager with each passing day for the life-giving rays of the sun to return.

A November moon shines over icebergs frozen stationary in the Inglefield Bredning Fjord. The sun set on October 26, and will not rise again until February 17.

Sunday Surprise

While in Qaanaaq preparing for our departure, I decided to go to the church service on Sunday morning. As is true for most Greenlandic communities, the church is located in the center of the village. The church bells start ringing at 9:00 a.m., even though the service is at 10 a.m. The ringing gets all the huskies in town howling—on key! The bell is rung again at 9:30 a.m. This gives the families time to dress and make the climb to the church.

It is still dark in February, even though it is late morning. The church was small, with room for around seventy-five people. There were only about twenty people there when I arrived and they were all sitting in the back. It seemed odd that all the church benches in the front half were empty and the back full. I thought it must be because the Inuit people are often a bit shy and very humble. The pastor didn't seem to mind speaking loudly to his congregation, so all in back could hear. As I listened, I noticed, just behind the altar, a giant painting of Jesus with two Inuit children in his lap. But it was a somewhat unusual painting.

Since it is very cold in Qaanaaq, the congregation thought it strange that pictures of Jesus always showed him with bare feet and sandals. This just would not do in north Greenland, so they got together and decided to paint socks on their Jesus' feet. It makes quite an impression the first time you see this painting on the wall at the front of the church.

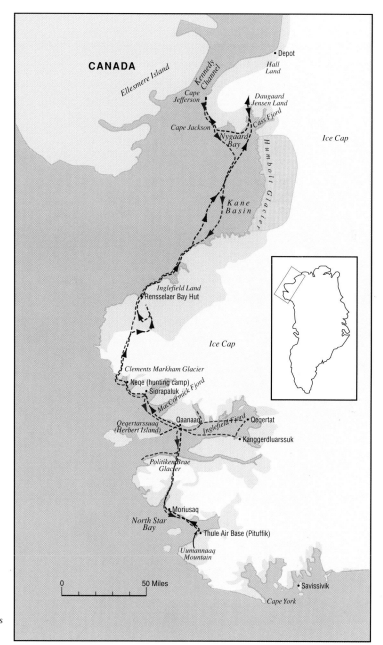

This map gives an overview of our main routes during the dog sledge campaign.

Our dogs must adapt to the most hostile weather on Earth. They allow themselves to be buried by the snow for extra insulation.
In the old days, harnesses were made of bearded seal hide; then they were made of cotton lamp wick; today, we use nylon webbing.

January 8, 1998

For the first time in fifteen years, I'd begun to think I had lost the spirit for the Arctic. But now, on the last flight of the week by chopper to Qaanaaq, it had come back. Wearing earmuffs to reduce the hum of the rotor blades, I looked down on the fjord ice below and saw the lights of Moriusaq in the distance. It is the closest Inuit hunting community to Thule Air Base. The full moon had lit up the stranded icebergs, frozen in place until spring's thaw. The surrounding hills, steep to the coast and partially snow covered, were highlighted by shadows cast by the moon. We touched down in Qaanaaq and I was reunited with John, who had been given the name "Ujuut" by the Inuit during my absence.

John showed me where our dogs were located and I went to get acquainted with them. They are a motley crew, assembled from some five separate teams. Some of them are old, some young, some wild and some skittish. Tyson and Holyfield, the battling brothers, were not much more agreeable than when I had last seen them. Given the chance, they would fight and push the other dogs off their food. We have our work cut out for us to make them ready for the trip, but I feel that we have the makings of a good team.

Dogs need to be handled with a great deal of respect and caution. The owner needs to handle the team with authority, the dogs knowing that he or she is the "alpha."

They are not pets, and can be extremely dangerous if left to run free in packs or when they are hungry. During my time in Greenland, I heard of several maulings and the death of a women who was walking between houses in the village. Before the tether law came into effect in both Canada and Greenland, all loose dogs were shot except whelping mothers and pups under six months old. Many children were killed by dogs, with only bits and pieces of fur parkas and pants left to be found. Kids are still taught to carry a stick with them even though the dogs are tethered.

British polar explorer Wally Herbert had a near-fatal experience while running his team on a long journey. Walking ahead of his team without his whip, he tripped over a piece of ice. Sensing his vulnerability, his dogs attacked. Wally curled up in a ball to protect his face and abdomen. His heavy fur pants and parka afforded him a temporary shield from the canine teeth. After an intense initial assault, the dogs pulled back to assess the damage they had inflicted, before resuming the attack. Given that single opportunity, Wally sprang up—sore, bruised, and more than a little unsettled—and hurriedly retrieved his whip from the back of the sledge. The dogs, seeing the tables had turned, grudgingly accepted a return to the established order.

Proper diet is as important for the dogs as it is for John and me. Extra fat is given to them in the extreme cold for needed calories while working hard. Feeding the dogs is usually done in the evening. In the summer, when it is warm and the dogs aren't working, they are fed meat or dried fish every third day. In winter, when it's not too cold and the dogs aren't working, they are fed every other day. In the winter, while they are working, they are fed every day.

Still too young for work, this five-month-old pup enjoys his freedom around the village while making his home, as many do, under a storage building.

Seal meat is always preferred as an all-around food for dogs when it is in ample supply.

During extreme cold and hard work, especially on extended journeys, walrus meat and skin is also good for the dogs. Walrus skin, which is about a half-inch thick with a little fat left on it, is cut into thin strips. The hide is so tough that the strips need to be thin, around an inch or so, and six inches long so the dogs can swallow them whole. This high protein, high calorie food, will keep the dogs satisfied for a long time.

Our hut on the edge of the village consists of a remodeled 20x40–foot shipping container. This type of large-scale "recycling" is common practice in the Arctic to satisfy the need for temporary and portable housing.

January 13

We had a three-day training run down the Inglefield Fjord east of Qaanaaq. The first objective was to put some miles on the dogs, building their muscles for the long journey to start on February 14, and to get them to work as a cohesive team. This means working out their aggression and allowing them the chance to establish a pecking order. Though John has kept the dogs in good shape during my absence, they were not responding well to commands. They were receiving too many separate and varying signals—in English, Danish, Australian, Inuit—and becoming confused. These dogs are smart, but not multi-lingual! We decided on seven basic and easy-to-pronounce Inuit commands already familiar to the dogs, each one telling them to stay, go, go fast, go right, go left, come, or stop.

The second objective was to hone our travel skills. The more apparent reason for the trip was to retrieve meat from three narwhals cached last fall at the end of the fjord. The 90-mile round trip would be with our Inuit friends Aaron Duneq from Qaanaaq and Asiajuk Sadorana, one of the few residents of Kangerdlugssuag, a three-house village down the fjord. Aaron, in his late forties, and Asiajuk, in his late fifties, each drove his own dog team.

We traveled through polar night without even the moon to guide us because of the pujuq (ice fog). Somehow we managed, and our eyes became adjusted enough to the dark to make out our route. There were only different shades of darkness to differentiate one thing from another. Feeling chilled by the polar night air, we would run alongside the sledge about every 10 minutes to build up steam. Even though it's dark and the dogs need a lot more work, we are making miles and it feels good to be traveling by sledge again.

The next day we made it to the stone caches and found the meat undisturbed by polar bears. The faint odor that came from beneath the rocks did attract a fox that then had the misfortune to be caught in one of Asiajuk's traps. (The valuable fur will be incorporated into clothing by his wife, Benigne.) It took four of us three hours under the light of a lantern, using picks and pry bars, to remove the meat from the rocks. The meat had the sweet pungent odor of slight fermentation. We chopped up some with the axe for the dogs and used our knives to shave off small, thin, frozen pieces for us to eat raw. We transported the rest of the meat by dog sledge back to Qaanaaq—some 800 pounds in all.

Large rock caches like this one are used to stockpile narwhal and walrus meat to be retrieved later in the winter. The rocks protect the meat from direct sunlight and ravenous foxes.

February 10

We did our final training run with the dogs to Qeqertarrsuaq (Herbert Island), which is a landmark that dominates the view from Qaanaaq. It was like stepping back in time when we pulled into the village. Dog teams and sledges were parked out in front of the small houses, the tiny windows illuminated from within by kerosene lamps. Seal carcasses, hung from the meat racks and out of the reach of the dogs, showed that the recent hunt had been successful.

Dog Teams

The qimmit (sled dog) is a powerful draft animal and hunting companion for the Inuit. The males are very sturdy, weighing in at around 80 pounds, while the females are quite a bit lighter, around 60 pounds. The dogs are used to pull the sledge and gear over various obstacles en route to hunting locations. In addition, the qimmit is used for its sense of smell to find seal breathing holes and to follow polar bear tracks.

Currently, most teams in the Thule district consist of between 10 and 14 dogs. These are considered large teams, and are supported by good hunting and a large supply of walrus and seal in the area. Commercial dog food and dried fish can also be purchased for the dogs at a reasonable cost.

At the turn of the century, a family's team consisted of only 5 to 7 dogs. When traveling with all their belongings from seasonal camps, the family helped the dogs push and pull the sledge and large load. The modern increase in dog numbers is partly due to better techniques for hunting and fishing in recent years, as well as the availability of commercial dog food.

In north Greenland, puppies are allowed to run free until 6 months of age, when their apprenticeship as a sledge dog begins.

On the move to Siorapaluk, the northernmost village in the world, to begin our expedition farther north. We use the tried-and-tested methods of the Inuit and run our dogs in the fan formation.

We had coffee in one of the warm little huts belonging to Mamarut Kristiansen and his wife Tekumeq. Mamarut shook his head and laughed when he recognized Tyson and Holyfield scrapping over their food. Inside, a frozen seal lay thawing on the floor next to the stove. Two female dogs and their newborn puppies lay in the entrance. The house was small to make it easy to heat, the walls only 6½-feet high.

During our visit, it was interesting to find out that this was the same house in which Wally Herbert and his wife Marie lived during their one-year stay in the village.

February 14

Although it was a cold and windy departure from Qaanaaq, we had a warm sendoff from our Danish and Greenlandic friends. We are finally on our way to Siorapaluk, 39 miles away, the first stop on our expedition north. Our sledges are heavy with the equipment and supplies that will keep John, me, and the dogs alive for the next month until we reach our first depot at Rensselaer Bay. The hundreds of hours of fund-raising, preparation, and training have taken their toll on me. Now I want to leave all the headaches behind and get down to the basics of life. No bills, no taxes, no job worries—for now, that is. Nothing to consider except surviving the trials of polar travel.

February 15, Siorapaluk

As we arrived, most of the community came out on the ice to welcome us. It was great to see these wonderful people of the north with their wide smiles on bronze-colored faces. The children were

After only 2 days on the ice cap north of Siorapaluk, we are already bored with the surroundings. Navigation becomes difficult with no landmarks to follow.

This is the south view from the hill behind our hut in Qaanaaq.
Directly across the fjord is the Politiken Brae Glacier and sledge route to Thule Air Base.

climbing and playing on our sledges while the adults and elders examined and commented on our equipment. With the help of friends living in Siorapaluk, Peter Duneq (Aaron's brother) and Alinguaq (overseer of the local store), we soon had settled our dogs and purchased a supply of walrus meat. Once comfortable, the stories started, and went on into the night . . .

They began with talk of walrus and polar bear hunting. Many of the hunters were out some miles north of the village hunting aaveq (walrus) near the flow edge. Bear hunting begins here when the weather warms up and the month of April brings more light. I am told that when a bear is hunting its main diet of seal, it will scratch away at the ice surrounding a seal breathing hole, enlarging it with its powerful claws. Then it will lie there, spread out on the ice, ready to snatch the surfacing seal with a swipe of its massive paw. Amazing!

February 16

Today we have been told that the ice near the Clements Markham Glacier is still too thin for us to begin.

February 18

As we finally departed today from Siorapaluk, Aaron, Asiajuk, and his wife Benigne joined us, making a caravan of 3 dog sledges and 49 dogs. They will help us transport some of our equipment and provisions over the 175 miles north to Cass Fjord and then return to Qaanaaq. If the conditions are good they will hunt bear and seal along the way. Benigne will help prepare any seal or bear skins that the hunters may acquire and repair any worn spots in their fragile fur clothing. Benigne wears a beautiful blue fox parka while her husband sports one of caribou. Both wear bear pants for traveling, as is the custom with polar Eskimos. Polar bear pants last up to five years, even with continual use, and are amazingly warm. They also provide a good "cushion" while riding the sledge.

At noon, stopping for tea and a short rest as all hunters do while on the trail, we finally saw the sun after its absence for four months! What a lovely thing it is!

Even though the temperature is far below zero, you could still imagine warmth on your face, and it lifted our spirits.

We continued to travel and managed to make 25 miles to the hunting camp known as Neqe, which is frequented mostly by walrus hunters during the late fall through late spring.

February 19

Although this leg of the expedition has already officially started, I feel the adventure of it really began today with our ascent of Clements Markham Glacier. The great explorers—Rasmussen and Freuchen—traveled this glacier on their pursuits north, exploring the unknown. We managed to ascend half of the glacier today and will ice our runners for tomorrow's steep climb.

Our tent and sledge are almost completely buried with hard-packed snow. The strain on the tent had us worried as the deafening wind accelerated to 100 mph.

Icing of the runners reduces friction caused by extreme cold or heavy loads and will help us and the dogs get to the summit. This process requires melting lots of ice for water so that cotton fiber can be soaked in it and applied to the runners. The warm, wet cotton fiber is rolled out onto the runners and molded by hand, making cracking sounds as it adheres around the lip of the burning cold plastic and steel shoeing. After it has hardened, this new "shoe" of ice is then scraped smooth with a sharp knife, removing any humps or rough spots. To finish the process, cold water is applied while rubbing a piece of bear hide back and forth over the area. The result is a firm, even layer of thin ice that glides better than any other known material. This is an agonizing process, and our hands are nearly as frozen as the shoeing when we are finished.

February 20

A major blizzard started last evening and we are only alive because of our tent. The wind today is in excess of 100 mph and all my attempts to go outside to better secure the tent and check on the dogs have failed. I crawled on my hands and knees just outside of the tent, trying to move snow blocks and gear bags tighter against the flapping nylon. It was pointless. The wind just blew the 45-pound bags aside as fast as I could put them in place.

Even with goggles, I mostly had to feel my way around the perimeter of the tent. I knew if I lost my hold on the rope tiedowns and became disoriented, I could freeze to death only a few feet from the tent.

Attempting to stand and being blown off my feet would surely have been suicide.

I could hear a very faint whine, indicating that the dogs weren't having any fun either. After what seemed like an eternity, I finally found the entrance to the tent. Snow had penetrated every square inch of my clothing, leaving snowdrifts in all my pockets and melting snow around my neck and wrists.

"What did you see?" John asked.

"Absolutely nothing," was all I could reply.

February 21

Last night was a waking nightmare with the feeling of being buried alive as the tent walls came in closer and closer with the weight of the snow.

Our floor space has been reduced to half. Unable to go outside to shovel away the snow, we had to put our backs against the wall of the tent and our feet against the other side to keep it from collapsing under the weight.

No going outside to relieve ourselves. We use a bottle and dump it just outside the tent flap.

As we huddle in our modern tent, with its aerodynamic design to minimize the impact of high winds, we are wondering how our Inuit friends are faring in their larger, more exposed canvas tent. By late afternoon, there was a brief lull, and Aaron came to give us a report: The two 2-inch-diameter tent poles that held up their tent had snapped during the night, leaving them huddled under flapping canvas. As spin-drifted snow entered through the torn tent, their fur clothing had become wet, leaving them increasingly cold and fatigued. They were going to have to do something quickly to improve their situation.

Resorting to the old ways, the two men were able to build an igloo between gusts and managed to move into it just before the storm rose again to its earlier fury. During the same brief lull, John and I attempted to remove some of the compacted snow that had accumulated around the outside of the tent.

We also know that our selection of a campsite has aggravated

During a lull in the storm at the Clements Markham Glacier, Aaron and Asiajuk build an emergency igloo. The previous 3 days were spent under flapping canvas and in wet clothes because the wind collapsed their tent poles.

our situation. The glacier is flanked on both sides by sheer cliffs and our camp is in the middle, as if sitting on a massive frozen river at the bottom of a huge canyon. This creates a wind tunnel effect and accelerates the storm to gale force. John and I were aware of the situation, but the Inuit seemed unconcerned. It just goes to show that even people who live in this environment all of their lives can make misjudgements.

The sun barely crests the horizon at noon during this time of year. This made for short travel days and setting camp in the dark.

February 22

It is now day four of the storm. There is no letup in sight. John and I had to sleep fully clothed in our sleeping bags, prepared for the possibility that our tent might be ripped from over us. In such an event, being undressed and unprepared would have spelled the end for the expedition, and us.

The wind against the ripstop nylon of the tent creates a deafening sound. John and I can only communicate by yelling, even though we are only inches apart. Earplugs fashioned from foam chewed off my sleeping pad were necessary just to get some sleep. Our shelter has held up so far, but we are wondering just how much abuse it can take before failing. During the night, the lantern swung so violently from the apex of the tent that it finally fell to the floor in pieces.

Our Inuit friends have exhausted their fuel supply and are getting cold from sleeping in their fur clothing which is now full of frost and fine snow. We gave them two of our emergency stoves and fuel, hoping to get them by until the storm diminishes.

We are concerned now that if the storm doesn't let up pretty soon, all of us will be lost to Mother Nature.

February 23

It's the fifth day of the storm and the wind is still averaging 75 mph.

We've decided to make a retreat down the glacier as soon as the wind subsides a little, even if darkness is approaching. This decision is not a matter of choice. Our Inuit friends are freezing to death because of their damp clothing, and all the dogs have ice balls on their fur coats. But to make a retreat in this kind of weather will be extremely dangerous. We could easily get lost and fall victim to the blinding snow and frostbite in half an hour.

Our intent is to follow a moraine ridge on the west side of the glacier down to a small hunting hut located at the bottom. By following the moraine, our chance of getting lost is reduced. We will leave John's sledge and some provisions behind, hook all 21 dogs to my sledge, and head down the glacier with rope brakes thrown over each runner to slow our descent.

During a storm, I had to guide our dogs on a single sled back down the dangerous descent of Clements Markham Glacier.
Following a moraine to keep our bearings, we managed to find a safer place to camp.

Sledges

Our Qamutit (dog sledge) design comes from the Polar Inuit (Eskimos) of Greenland for use in rough sea ice and for carrying heavy loads. When fully loaded, a sledge can handle weights up to 1,000 pounds which can be pulled easily by 14 dogs. Sledges on average are about 14 feet long and 3 feet wide. The 3-foot-tall stanchions lashed to the back of the sledge are used as handles in maneuvering or pushing the sledge.

The average sledge can be loaded with a maximum weight equal to the weight of the dogs. For example, if you have 8 dogs that weigh an average of 70 pounds each, a total of 560 pounds can be put on the sledge—including the driver. Dogs can pull their own weight daily with a rest every fifth to seventh day. A team of good dogs will run at about 5 to 6 miles per hour and can cover up to 50 miles in a single day. The Inuit try not to overwork the dogs when hauling heavy loads in extreme cold, running them an average of 5 to 7 hours each day. This allows the dogs to take good care of the pads of their feet.

The dogs' harnesses are made of ¾-inch-wide nylon webbing and sewn together using nylon thread. When making harnesses, all measurements are calculated using fingers, hands, and arm lengths. The dog traces, the long lines they are tied to the sled with, are generally over three full arm lengths long. This is around 18 feet. One or two leader dogs are sometimes given an additional arm length of rope, so they are ahead of the rest of the team.

Being inside a ping-pong ball is an accurate description of what it's like to move in a "white-out." With no depth perception, we are constantly worried about falling into crevasses or tripping in depressions while walking or skiing.

Shortly after starting, we lost what little light we had. We now had not only the storm to contend with, but darkness as well. Though we couldn't see Aaron or Asiajuk and Benigne ahead of us, we could make out sledge tracks here and there to guide us. On occasion, I had to get down on all fours to spot a sledge runner track in the hard-packed snow.

We then had to cross over some smaller moraine hills, the sledge getting caught on the rocks and digging deep into our plastic runners. After several minutes of yelling and pushing to encourage the dogs, we managed to inch the sledge forward. Around a final bend approaching more level terrain, I got my leg caught between the sledge and a huge boulder. I had immediate thoughts of a compound fracture as the strength of 21 dogs squeezed my leg flat. Luckily, the sledge caught on a smaller rock just ahead and I escaped with only a scrape and a bruise.

The thing that I fear the most is the ever-present possibility of a major medical emergency like appendicitis or compound fracture. If something like that happened now, in the midst of this storm, it could be days before a rescue flight could reach us, and then it might be too late.

We finally made the hut—exhausted, cold, and grateful to be alive. After running with 21 dogs in the dark and in a storm for several hours, I was left with the agonizing task of untangling each of the 21 tightly woven traces that connect the back of each dog's harness to the front of the sledge before I could enjoy the warmth of the hut. With near-frozen fingers, it was the worst 8-foot knot I ever had to undo. Once the dogs were separated, I gathered each by its 18-foot line and tethered them all for the night.

We can take only 15-minute breaks for a warm drink from the thermos and some high-calorie snacks before the cold creeps back into our bodies.

Pups

I saw a funny thing today. A young boy, about seven years of age, was "playing trucks" in the sand. But he wasn't using the usual toy trucks, he was using some young puppies! The fat and furry little pups were only a few weeks old, and had only recently gained their sight. When gently handled by the boy, they just grunted as they were moved about. And their mother nearby didn't seem to mind at all.

Female dogs are usually bred in the late winter so the pups and new mother do not have to go through a hard winter shortly after birth. If there were new pups born in the winter, it would also require the hunter to provide more meat and care to the dogs. Pups that are born and fed well through summer will grow to be big and strong.

By the time November comes around, the dogs have reached seven months of age and can be harnessed and taken on short runs with the adult dogs. Sometimes, the young dogs are just allowed to run with the adults unharnessed. By prime sledging conditions in March and April they will be working with the rest of the team. Once the dog is about a year old, it is fitted with a custom harness that some wear from then on, winter and summer.

Almost all of the vacant land between the homes in the village is used by sledge dog families taking a well-deserved break from last winter's work.

February 24

The hut measures about 12 feet square and smells of kerosene and walrus fat. To us it is a castle with the finest facilities. The snow that virtually buries the tiny structures creates a nice sound barrier against the howling wind. The warmth of our Primus stove fills the hut, and we are drying our clothing and laughing about the past days of bad luck. Aside from having to shovel snow away from the door every hour to keep from being trapped, the day has been total relaxation. The wind here is much less and the dogs are now getting a chance to clean their coat free of snow and sleep comfortably with a belly full of food.

After the storm completely cleared, we thoroughly checked the dogs and found that all 49 were fine. It just confirms the hardiness of the Inuit dog. I have never known a healthy one to die of the cold or a storm. It's almost unbelievable how well they manage.

Aaron, Asiajuk, and Benigne have elected not to go on to Cass Fjord with us. Badly shaken by their experience in the storm, they have decided that it's too early in the season and they have had enough of storms!

The storm subsided this afternoon and we said goodbye to our friends as they left to return to Qaanaaq. John and I feel much more alone. We'd been glad for the Inuits' company and for their help but now we were faced with having to carry all of our supplies between the two of us. Since we will be combining our two teams into one eventually, we had to send five of our dogs back with them now, much sooner than we planned. Twenty-one dogs in a single team would be too much to handle and feed. This will mean slower progress on top of the six precious days we have already lost to the storm.

Protected by long guard hairs and soft downy underfur, one of the dogs, named Quick, curls up to keep his feet and nose warm.

At the same time, we have been heartened by our recent experience. We feel more confidence in ourselves and our equipment. If we could survive that blizzard with everything intact, what could stop us?

February 25

Have you ever had one of those days when no matter how you open the matchbox, it's upside down and the matches end up in the snow? Today was one of those days.

Dog Training

For a team to function efficiently, there are several basic commands the dogs must be trained to understand.

"a - a" . . . . means stop
"ah - ah" . . . . means come
"huk - huk" . . . . means go
"hookwa - hookwa" . . . . means go fast
"atsuk" or "et - et" . . . . . means turn right
"hargu - hargu" . . . . . . .means turn left
"aquitsin" . . . . means lay down

In addition to verbal commands, the hunter carries his iperataq (whip) with him at all times to further control the dogs. It has a 2½-foot handle with approximately 25 feet of tapered, bearded seal skin. The whip is used in conjunction with voice commands. For example, if the hunter wants to turn his team to the left, he cracks his whip to the right of the dogs and yells "Hargu!"

The whip is used to break up dogfights that might otherwise leave the dogs lame or dead. It is also used to keep the dogs sitting while undoing the traces from the sledge, to untangle the traces, or to keep the dogs from running over a cliff or onto thin ice.

My friend Jens Danielsen and his family nearing the village Moriusaq to hunt utoq (seals) on the ice. We first met in 1991 while I was crossing the Canadian Arctic by dog team. He was doing the same trip, but from the opposite direction.

We left our little hut and began to ascend the glacier. We passed the remains of the camp where we had spent the storm—broken tent stakes, snow blocks, and hundreds of dog turds in a 50-yard radius. On our way by, we divided the sixteen dogs into two teams and picked up John's sledge again.

For the remainder of the day, we pushed and hauled our heavy loads to within a mile of the summit. The windstorm had gouged large, 4-foot-high waves into the snow of the glacier, and crossing them caused our fully loaded sledges to repeatedly overturn. It took all of our effort to right them again. Progress could only be made by hooking all the dogs to one sledge and relaying them. We would advance the first sledge about half a mile, unhook the dogs, return to the second sledge, and repeat the process.

Just before we stopped to make camp in the approaching darkness, I was using my iperataq (steering whip) to keep the dogs away from a crevass and managed to catch my eye with it. Dropping to the ground howling in pain, I felt certain it was serious. This was not the place to be partially blinded. Distracted, I carelessly left my whip lying on the snow and Holyfield, known for his sneakiness, wolfed down ten feet of it like spaghetti!

While setting up camp, I stumbled twice into small crevasses that I otherwise would have seen. John put some tetracaine and salve on my eye to ease the pain and covered it. Hopefully I will be able to sleep.

February 26, made 5 miles

When I woke up this morning, vision with my injured eye was foggy, but it seemed improved. The area we camped in is peppered with crevasses, and I had been concerned about the dogs slipping into hidden ones during the night. But all was well.

I was completely exhausted from having to relay supplies to the glacier's summit.

Ascending to the ice cap's plateau.

February 27

This day went much smoother. We iced the runners and the dogs had an easier time pulling the sledges. We crossed some monster crevasses after probing each snowbridge with our ice chisel to be confident it would hold. These crevasses would easily swallow a Caterpillar tractor.

It was sunny and cold with temperatures again near -36°F — the first clear day since we left. From the ice cap's plateau we are able to see the majestic mountains of Canada's Ellesmere Island some 70 miles to the west. I sure enjoyed the day. The dogs were happy too, after having two double feedings in the last two days.

As we approached the end of the day, I looked back to see John's team coming through a cloud of ice vapor created by heat from the dogs' bodies. The vapor was so thick that I could hardly make out John at the back of the sledge.

The low-lying sun on this cold day produced mirages on the distant ice and horizon, surrounding us in an illusion of huge, sheer cliffs and mountains.

Before entering the warmth of the tent we remove our outer anorak, shaking away the frost that accumulates between the layers. We in turn brush from each other's back and arms the frost that has formed from the day's exertions. The smaller items—frozen neck gaiters, boot liners, socks, and handwear—are hung over a drying string attached to the ceiling of the tent. Unfortunately, there is never enough heat to get them completely dry, but every bit helps. We knock the frost out of our articles of fur clothing with a stick and store them under the sledge cover away from the hungry dogs. When hungry, the dogs will try to eat

While we packed to depart, two of our dogs, Aten and his brother Alingnik came over, rubbing and pushing back and forth against my legs like cats. I wondered how they could be so content and happy under these difficult circumstances. I found myself drawing energy from them for the coming day.

The 600-foot cliffs that flank the glacier are rust in color and seem just able to hold back the ice cap's plateau, which hangs over the summit. We finished our second day of relaying the sledges, sweating at -36°F as we pushed and righted our loads.

most anything—nylon harnesses, skin clothing and boots, and pieces of rope. When not hungry, they gnaw on frozen dog turds just for fun. Anything that can conceivably be chewed needs to be lashed down under the sledge cover. This point was driven home today when John left his cherished caribou fur mitts hanging over the back of the sledge. Unattended for just a moment, sly Holyfield devoured the thumb and a portion of the fingers off one mitt. Cursing, John ran and retrieved his damaged mitt, knowing he would have to spend precious sleep time tonight mending it.

February 28

A moderate east wind has picked up and created a small ground blizzard. We are staying put today.

I have been a bit crabby with John lately. I'm sure it's due to the stress of being cooped up with each other in the tents during the long storms we've had. John and I are very different, but that's partly why we make a good team. He is easygoing and can maintain a happy-go-lucky attitude in the face of adversity. This is my first requirement for a team member. He is also better than I am with small details, is a hard worker, and is eager to learn.

A source of conflict between us is my feeling that John is too slow and methodical in many of the daily camp routines and has difficulty improvising. I have chided him, saying that he cannot improvise without the manual. He might take the time to find a hammer when a rock would work just fine. Some of it is me being impatient, but it's hard to be patient at 50 below. Under normal circumstances, it's been a good-natured give-and-take. But our circumstances aren't normal, and this has become a sore spot between us.

Stopping for a brief rest and to do some reconnaissance of the route ahead, we ponder our options.

85

Limited to only a few hours of light in early March, we must carry on in the dark, sledding north
along the icefoot (a flat area between the rough, pressured sea ice and shore).

But if asked whether I would have picked someone else for this project, my answer would be an emphatic "No!" John has been irreplaceable in the preparations of this project. His dedication is without question.

March 1

It's still storming on the plateau. Our food and fuel are holding OK, but I have thoughts of our depot at the Rensselaer Bay hut. It was placed there by chopper last fall. Could bears have gotten into it? Bears are not common in that area, but it only takes one. John assures me that the hut is sound and our depot should be intact. We both hope he's right.

March 2

We made an easy descent off the plateau to a river valley in Inglefield Land. The snow cover is thin to nonexistent. Steel runner shoes or very thick plastic ones are a must in this rocky country. We traveled down a dry river bed for about 11 hours and are exhausted.

Our position is 78°31′North, 70°36′West.

March 3

Today we sought a river valley that would lead us to the Rensselaer Bay hut and depot. We made runs down two impassable canyons in that attempt. Failing, we had to return to camp. In the process we collapsed the wooden stanchions on the back of the sledge when it turned completely upside down next to a huge rock where the snow had been removed by the wind. We figure

that we are one river system too far to the east and need to backtrack to get on the right one tomorrow.

Exhausted, John and I were kidding with each other saying we should quit all this training and begin the real expedition!

March 4

We got up early this morning in the hope of retracing part of our route, finding the right one, and reaching the hut. The runners took a real beating today on the rocks as we navigated for the correct river system.

With the temperature at -45°F and after more than 10 hours of traveling, we finally made the hut. I was feeling my age and then some.

It was a steep hill downward to the hut and we had to use both rope brakes to control our speed as we descended to the bay. The simple, box-shaped hut was built not long ago for polar bear hunters on extended journeys.

Rensselaer Bay is surrounded by 600-foot-high, tan-colored cliffs and is home to a herd of muskox that migrated over from Canada's Ellesmere Island, and a few Peary caribou, which are all white and smaller than their relatives from the south.

Like waves at sea frozen in time, the wind sculpts beautiful patterns in the snow around us.

March 8, made only 13 miles

John and I are becoming more efficient as we work together, taking less time setting up and breaking camp. In the evenings, after working together to erect the tent, John collects blocks of snow, glacial ice from a nearby berg, or salt-free, multi-year ice from the surrounding pack to be melted for drinking. He also takes care of the dogs. Multi-year ice is recognized by its rounded tops and consists of large pieces of sea ice left over from previous summer melts. Over time and cycles of melting, salt leaches out of the top, leaving freshwater ice.

I arrange the inside of the tent, heat water for thermoses, and fix dinner. In the morning, I wake up, get the stove going, and fix breakfast. Our routines have become automatic; we know what we need to do without saying anything. We've gotten skilled and efficient at what each of us does, and that makes a good team. But the hardest thing for me to do on the expedition is to get out of my sleeping bag at -50°F to get the stove going! Cold fuel containers give off vapor like dry ice when brought into a warm tent to fill stoves. The fuel, thickened and almost gelled from the cold, is difficult to ignite and must be handled with mittens to avoid cold burns.

When we enter our sleeping bags at night the inside of the bag is the same temperature as the outside air. It takes a supreme effort to slip into the cold nylon sack kicking our legs and moving our arms violently to bring warmth to the bag. Our feet, tucked away in extra thick insulated boot liners, are the last to warm up. Nights are spent rolling from side-to-back-to-side, trying to find a comfortable position, or lying awake with the

March 7

We left the hut after three days of much-needed rest. The sledges were each laden with 800 pounds of supplies for our 300-mile journey north to our next depot in Hall Land.

Today was the first time on the expedition that I wore all the clothing I have with me. It was -45°F here and a little more humid than high up on the ice cap where we were just a few days ago.

Our ration of Canadian whiskey was frozen rock hard in its nalgene bottle!

John helps push our sledge up to the icefoot after hours of hacking a road with picks through pressured shore ice.

Out of frustration and in hope of making better time, we combine our efforts, dogs, and supplies to one sledge.

uneasy thought of having heard something outside that might be a bear.

I was irritated last night that John was snoring again, a state often achieved before his head even reaches his rolled-up anorak pillow. I decided to apply a remedy that the Inuit use when there is a snorer in the tent.

"Hey John! Hey, did you hear that? I think there's a bear outside!" And while your partner intently listens for sounds of the marauder, you slip off to sleep.

Numerous times we have had to leave the warmth of our sleeping bags, grabbing the combination rifle/shotgun from the vestibule of the tent as we exited, to see if it really was a bear. We are always relieved to find it's usually just a loose dog digging around on the sledge and in need of tethering again. Then the whole process of warming up the bag starts all over. After a while, exhaustion and fatigue take over and you fall asleep to dreams of food.

March 11, -43°F

We are having a rest day today, and will switch to one sledge tomorrow in the hope of being more efficient. Our loads have been reduced over the last five days so we no longer need both sledges. We can combine the dogs into one large team. The sledge will weigh 1,200 pounds when we leave tomorrow, and icing of the runners will be a must in the morning. We chopped up John's sledge for firewood to melt snow and concocted a fatty stew for the dogs.

I have developed a cough and am having difficulty sleeping.

This, and frost falling loose from the tent ceiling and landing on my face, keeps me awake. I must sleep on my side in an attempt to control my coughing. Our tent is small and relatively easy to heat at night with our cookstove. It's around -5°F on the floor and 70°F on the ceiling—just warm enough to partially dry our frost-filled clothes. After 8 or 9 hours of traveling, you build up a lot of moisture in your clothing, so we try to dry out smaller items like footwear, handwear, and hats each night.

Have not been able to make radio contact with the outside. We wonder if the radio is broken. I miss Kelly a lot. When I think about her while I am in this state of mind it puts me in a terrible funk. We have 16 days of full rations left on the sledge, and hope we can make Hall Land before they run out.

Although we are eating 5,000 to 6,000 calories daily—which is like consuming the equivalent of three Thanksgiving dinners back home—we are still ravenously hungry at the end of the day.

March 14, -57°F, made 9 miles

Our sledge and skis refuse to glide at these temperatures. When I ski, I just shuffle my feet and it's only slightly better than walking.

Even though we wear fur ruffs around our hoods to protect our faces from the biting cold, and apply a lanolin/Vaseline-based cream to cheekbones, nose, and ears, we are each marked with a collage of scabs and frostbite, especially around the nostrils. Any exposed flesh freezes in seconds. John has developed quarter-sized rings of frostbite on his cheeks.

In order to prevent overheating and sweating during hard work or skiing, we remove our windshell anoraks. Here, John's frostbite is becoming evident.

I take a breather before continuing on skis along a welcomed flat and frozen lead just ahead of the dogs. Past days of cold, -57 degree temperatures and rough pack ice have taken their toll on us.

Due to the extreme cold, the baskets have broken off all but one of our ski poles. Our bindings, which performed flawlessly on earlier expeditions, are in shambles. They are being held together with parachute cord. The binding manufacturer apparently has changed to a different plastic resin composite for extruding the binding. I am so disgusted with our predicament, I would gladly pay $2,000 for a decent binding right now.

We can usually tell how cold it is by the volume of styrofoam-like squeaks the snow makes under ski and foot.

But the silver lining is the beautiful orange full moon tonight.

March 16, -34°F, made 21 miles

While stopping briefly for a snack we heard something odd. We couldn't figure it out. After some searching, we realized it was the tick of the second hand on a watch deep inside the sledge bag.

It's hard to believe how deathly quiet it can get out here. I remember Torben Diklev, director of the Thule Museum, once summed up the cold, vast silence of the Arctic by asking, "How can so much be so still?"

We are now seeing more of the sun. It stays just above the horizon as it rotates around us. Ellesmere Island, Canada, is clearly visible 60 miles away and bathed in red at night.

Ellesmere Island is separated from Greenland by the Kennedy Channel. Our plan is to get to the north of Kennedy Channel via an overland route through Daugaard Jensen Land.

We traveled down Nygaard Bay to the river valley that feeds it. The only maps produced of this area are 1:1,000,000 scale, and they provide absolutely no detail. The maps we used in south Greenland were 1:250,000.

After following the river for 6 miles, we sensed that it was leading to a dead end. I called for John to stop while I skied ahead to reconnoiter. I didn't have to go very far before I could see that it would be impossible to go any farther. The river narrowed into a gorge with sheer rock walls. The only conceivable route was along the bottom of the gorge and it was nothing but huge boulders.

Farther away was a series of frozen waterfalls for at least 3 miles. These icefalls were of polished ice between 50 and 100 feet in height. My heart sank at the sight before me, knowing we would have to retreat back through the difficult terrain we had just crossed.

We traveled in a ground blizzard and camped next to an iceberg in the bay. Tomorrow we will head for Kennedy Channel and Cape Jackson. After seeing the inland terrain firsthand, it was apparent that an attempt to cross land farther east up the Cass Fjord would have ended in failure. Our only option now is to make an attempt up the Kennedy Channel and pray that the ice is passable this year.

We have been avoiding this area from the start. It is well documented by past expeditions as an extremely difficult and sometimes impossible place to travel. We have no choice but to give it our best.

March 18, -39°F, made 17 miles

Each morning I can tell how cold it is by the difficulty I have lighting the stove. The film in my camera breaks when it's this cold and extra care has to be taken when advancing it. To avoid breaking the film, I often only shoot ¾ of the roll, then rewind it. It's easier to advance and rewind part of a roll than filling the whole spool. We also have problems with our lithium-powered light meters. The camera shutter is even slowed slightly in the cold, though we are using manual SLR cameras for most of our work.

It's getting lighter each day and soon we will no longer need our lantern. We spend much of our free time mending clothing and equipment that suffer from wear and tear. We still have been

A dog digs in the snow for a lost piece of food as the moon comes into view around the cape. We will soon no longer need our lantern, as the days become longer.

unable to make radio contact with the outside and are concerned that people may be getting worried about us. Every three days we have been sending pre-coded messages via Argos satellite that relate our position, air temperature, and status. Our sixteen messages range from message no. 1 stating "Traveling, everything OK" to message no. 8 stating "Medical emergency—life Threatening—need air rescue." We are transmitting regularly, but we are not sure if our office in Minnesota is receiving the messages. We can only assume that they are.

Each time our heavy sledge overturns in the rough pack ice, it takes an hour in the extreme temperatures—
with near-frozen hands—to up-right it, re-tie-down our supplies, and carry on.

The coastline on our way to Cape Jackson is rugged with sheer, 800-foot rock walls running parallel to our route. The cliffs are rust in color and flat on top. The base of the wall is buried in rocky rubble that extends all the way to the water's edge.

We were traveling next to the shore, dogs content with the routine, and John and I on skis, when I noticed an arctic fox coming in our direction a few hundred yards away. Though we were in the open, the fox appeared to be unaware of our presence. Neither did the dogs see it. It was not until they almost ran head-on into each other that the dogs bolted as if shot out of a cannon. The startled fox took off, the team and the 800-pound sledge in hot pursuit.

As if the sledge were empty, the fox and team headed up an almost vertical piece of pack ice.

The sledge came to a sudden halt looking as if it were sitting on its stanchions, dogs dangling from their traces and watching helplessly as the fox continued its run up the side of the cliff.

March 19, -39°F, made 16 miles

We skirted some very thin ice near Cape Jackson, a frozen-over "polynya." This is a normally open area of water produced by swift currents rounding a headland. Today, due to the extreme cold, a layer of thin ice had formed. I had been shuffling on foot in front of the dogs, checking each suspicious spot with a good jab of the ice chisel. On several occasions my chisel went completely through to the cold, black water, causing us to make a quick course change to firmer ice. My mind recoiled at the thought of being submerged in the icy waters at these temperatures.

With the presence of the thin ice we were seeing the tracks of many polar bears in search of seals, which congregate near thin ice because it is easier for them to make breathing holes or find openings in the ice. We were also encountering more and more pressure ridges—walls of ice several feet high that are pushed up by the collision of relatively flat pans of ice as they are driven about by the force of wind and current.

Judging by the way the dogs suddenly lifted their snouts to the sky, the scent of bear was surely in the air. They started to pick up the pace, but John and I still didn't see anything. Then we crossed a very fresh and very large track of an adult bear. Stopping the team, I went to examine the prints.

All at once the dogs bolted, with John hanging onto the sledge and our assortment of gear. Knowing the dogs had spotted a bear, I ran for all I was worth to catch up to John and our runaway sledge. A nasty scenario flashed through my head of our dogs in a bloody fight with a bear. The last thing we needed right now was some injured or dead dogs or having to shoot the bear in order to save the dogs. Nor could we afford to have the sledge damaged during the wild chase or the dogs somehow getting free of the sledge and chasing the bear into eternity.

Impassable pressured pack ice for as far as the eye can see at Cape Jefferson. Disheartened, I stare blankly across Kennedy Channel at the mountains of Ellesmere Island, Canada, knowing the only course is to turn back.

Grabbing the stanchions, I wiggled onto the sledge just as it became stuck on a pressure ridge. With my extra weight, the sledge and the dogs jerked to a screeching halt. When I finally looked up, I saw a yellowish 10-foot bear about 300 yards away. Even at that distance, it was massive, taking huge strides and quickly covering ground toward the protection of the jumbled pack ice—thankfully away from us!

This evening was the first time we were able to make radio contact since leaving the Rensselaer Bay hut. What a relief! We talked with Peter Duneq in Siorapaluk, who will relay to Kelly that we're OK.

March 20, -39°F—Kennedy Channel

We have been on the trail now for over a month and our bodies have become acclimatized to this brutal weather. We seem to handle the cold better each day, but just when we thought things might be getting a little better, the windchill factor went to -95°F.

John and I climbed a nearby cape to get a better view of the situation. Looking north from the summit, I tried not to believe my eyes—the worst pressure ridges and pack ice I had ever seen, stretching out endlessly to the horizon. My eyes watered from the killing cold of the north wind, the tears freezing instantly on my cheeks. I found myself wishing for a foxtail to hold in my teeth, an old Inuit trick for protecting the face when traveling into the wind.

For the first time, I felt like packing it in today. It's just too hard, too cold, too much, and too long. I'm unsure of what tomorrow might bring and our situation ahead appears grim. With the accumulated fatigue, and especially the hardships of today, I yelled at John for the first time. I told him he was the slowest person I'd ever met and I followed on to tell him that it felt good finally getting it off my chest. He replied in his characteristic accent—"Ha! Lonnie. You're impatient!" It was the response I had expected. Now, I feel badly for the outburst. Maybe we'll talk about it in the future, and maybe not. I think both of us realize it came more from stress than anything else.

The dogs' tempers seemed agitated as well and a nasty fight broke out between Igileraq and Tyson. The outcome left Igileraq with a nasty laceration where his paw hinged. I first applied an antibiotic cream and then Coban, an elastic/adhesive wrap, to stop the bleeding. Cut from the work load, he should be fine in a few days. We cannot afford any serious injuries at this point.

Caribou & Muskox

Tuktoo (caribou) meat can be eaten in many ways. It usually is boiled or can be dried into strips like jerky to be taken along on hunting excursions. Sometimes it is eaten in a raw, semi-frozen state where the only utensil needed is a knife. During the extreme cold, caribou fur is the primary source for making warm parkas. We used the durable hide from the legs to make our mittens for the expedition—it is hard to find a warmer mitt. These caribou "leggings" are also used to make the upper part of winter kamiks (boots).

Oomingmak (muskox) means "the animal with skin like a beard." Muskox have guard hair as long as 25 inches, which covers most of their short legs. This long hair covers a thick but soft layer of wool, that by weight is 8 times warmer than a domestic sheep's wool. Males can weigh around 600 pounds and females around 400. The muskox's unique horns grow downward and then outward near the jaw. They are used as defensive weapons against wolves and in fighting with other bulls. They are also used for rutting up vegetation.

Muskox are known for the instinctive circular defensive line formed by females and young bulls, with the calves in the center. The dominant bull patrols the outer perimeter. His primary job is to stand his ground and keep wolves from disbanding the herd and killing an unfortunate calf.

Primarily boiled, the meat has a strong wild taste and can be very tough. Most Inuit will eat muskox meat for variety in their diet, but they generally prefer caribou. Like caribou hide, muskox hide is scraped and utilized as a warm ground pad to sleep on during cold hunting trips. The wool, even softer than cashmere, is knitted and used today to make hats, shawls, and scarves.

A successful muskox hunt provides food for a hunter's family for many weeks to come.

Canine Dentistry

There are about 4 months during the warmer part of the year when dogs are not used for sledging. They are kept tethered to a rock or piece of ice by their 18-foot traces in groups of 3 to 5.

For the dogs to coexist peacefully, it is important that they were all brought up together, so that all the dogfights over hierarchy are over, and an alpha male and female have been established.

Also, the bottom and upper canine teeth need to be blunted slightly to reduce injury and death among the dogs during any remaining fights and squabbles over position. This also protects the hunter, or anyone else, from being severely injured from a dog bite or attack. The back molars are also blunted slightly to prevent the dog from chewing expensive harnesses and traces. If a hunter is out on the land far from the village, ruined harnesses could prove to be a serious problem.

The teeth are blunted just after the dog has gotten its permanent teeth and before winter. The process is usually done by two people, one armed with a small file or clippers, the other with two pieces of rope that go around the upper and lower jaws to hold the mouth open during the procedure. The job takes about five minutes and the dog comes out no worse for the wear.

Before the beginning of each sledge season, the hunter will also trim each dog's nails. Long nails can push back on the toes while the dog is pulling, making them sore. Long hair around the pads of the feet is also trimmed back to prevent ice balls from forming between the pads.

Breathing heavily, two brothers work hard together in the warmth of spring's 24-hour sunlight.

March 21, Cape Jefferson—80°20′ North 67°30′ West

This morning we managed to leave the icefoot (a narrow section of flat, landfast ice between the coast and the rugged sea ice) in an attempt to hack a road north through the ice with our pickaxes. We soon realized that this was futile. I guessed it would require six people and three dog teams ten hours of hacking a passage and relaying sledges to progress 1 to 3 miles. I climbed a nearby 50-foot piece of ice pressured up near shore to see if there was any hope or possibility of getting through.

Looking up the Kennedy Channel to the north, it was so blatantly obvious that we could go no farther that I broke down and cried. High walls of recently pressured ice marched north back-to-back, hopelessly blocking our path. I thought back on the three years of hard work getting to this point and about all our supporters pulling for us in the south. There was nothing I could do about it. I ran through my mental rolodex of options from fourteen years of arctic experience and could not come up with a successful solution to what I was seeing before me. A cloud of failure descended over me.

It was one of the most difficult days of my life. We had to make decisions today about the future of the project. We talked at length about our options, and none of them suited us. But we had to decide soon as both food and fuel were running short. We talked briefly about a high route up and over the Greenland ice cap, but by rule of the Danish Polar Center, ice cap travel before April 15 is prohibited. Even if we were willing to proceed in violation of this rule, we would consume precious time scouting new routes up and down the ice cap and would have to cross dangerous crevasse fields in the process. Travel would be unacceptably slow, and we would run out of supplies short of our next depot.

Sometimes the sea ice and icefoot would be completely pressured and jumbled to the steep coastline, leaving us only one option: to hack a road through the rubble.

Another option we discussed was pickup by chartered aircraft and dropoff at our next depot, then carry on as planned. This would add about $6,000 to our already substantial debt. It also contradicts the basic concept of the project—using only traditional modes of transportation. This has been a prime motivation for us and to do differently would take away from the credibility of the expedition and our commitment to it.

We have also decided not to signal for an airlift/rescue unless there is a threat of imminent loss of life to us or the dogs.

This option would end the dog sledge campaign entirely, marring our previous accomplishments. Besides, any rescue effort would most likely come from the Canadian side, and would leave us and our dogs stranded in some Canadian outpost with a handful of disgruntled polar scientists.

It was clear to John and me that our best recourse was to backtrack the 325 grueling miles to Siorapaluk on what remained of our food and fuel. This was a disheartening idea, knowing that we were only 125 miles from our Hall Land depot to the north and now had to go nearly three times the distance on our dwindling supplies. We could not expect any outside help in our efforts to return to Siorapaluk. All we knew is that it would take a superhuman effort to get there before our stores ran out.

We made 21 miles by early evening on the first day of the return trip and camped back at Cape Jackson.

March 22, Cape Jackson

We are dreading the inevitable hardships of the trip back. The days spent getting here are still fresh in our minds.

The thin ice on which we are traveling (called "rime") is perfectly flat, but the top is laced with salt and causes drag on my skis and the sledge. By the end of 20 miles, the dogs, John, and I are beat. John's ski bindings broke early on from the extreme cold, so he has been skijouring with the sledge for support or running alongside.

We need to find an old pan of ice to camp on tonight so the dogs have fresh snow to eat. They are becoming dehydrated from licking the salt ice on which we've been traveling the last few days. The bottom line is, if the dogs are not feeling well, you're not going anywhere. As a rule, dogs should never run on salt-laced snow or ice for more than 2 to 3 days in a row.

John and I have been pondering the near future and considering what our objectives should be if we make it back to the home of the Polar Inuit. We know that we would have a tremendous opportunity to travel with these people as they move back and forth to their hunting grounds by dog sledge. We could visit all the remote villages of the district and learn more about the lives and lifestyles of these fascinating people. This plan would still require hundreds of miles of sledging, but our dogs are good and the equipment is repairable.

Over the years, the Inuit people have been the main motivation for all my arctic journeys. The opportunity to live and travel with them during dog sledging season could quite possibly prove to be more rewarding than our initial objective. This prospect has brightened our outlook and now helps push us onward, back to the south.

March 23, -40°F, made 15.5 miles

The cold weather is causing considerable drag on the sledge runners, making it hard on the dogs. When it's this cold, the chemistry of the snow turns it granular and abrasive like sandpaper. We used up all the cotton for icing the runners many days ago. We've tried to improvise, using any available fabric from unused shirts and socks in an effort to find a material that will adhere to our runners so they can be iced. We spent a couple hours melting water and sizing fabric to fit the runners just to find out after the application that it just wouldn't work. I gave in and shaved the plastic runners as smooth as I could with my carpenter's plane. There isn't a whole lot of plastic left after our overland rock crossing early in the trip, but there should be enough on them to get us to Siorapaluk.

It's starting to cloud over now. We're hoping it will bring warmer weather and better sledging.

March 24, -36°F, made 11 miles

My nightmares of having to cross Kane Basin again through the awful pack ice and deep snow proved to be unfounded today. By climbing a high iceberg, I was able to see an opening to the south, just a few miles east of our previous northbound track. The snow was still quite deep, but the surface was relatively flat and unbroken. It was a welcomed opportunity to conserve what little energy we and the dogs have left. We are all tired and in need of a good night's sleep. In these extremes, we are only capable of about 7 hours of travel each day. When it warms up later in the spring, one can consistently travel 10 hours each day. People and dogs

These sun-bleached narwhal vertebra have been picked clean long ago by arctic foxes.

A frosty haze rises from the dogs' bodies in the extreme temperatures. Sometimes it's so thick I can't see John at the rear at all.

at the hut in Rensselaer Bay before crossing Inglefield Land and the ice cap.

Skiing out in front of the dogs mile after mile, the rhythm makes my mind wander—from thoughts of food, to what's ahead of us, to green grass, and back to food again. I can actually taste my mother's barbecued ribs! How wonderful it would be to have a good hot soak in a tub!

I can see land now on the other side of Kane Basin, and the cape we left several days ago. The sight of land gives us the encouragement of better days to come.

March 25, -35°F, made 18 miles

While skiing along and doing a little daydreaming, I spotted a black object on the ice several hundred yards away. I kept my eye on it to see if it was moving. Of course, if you look at anything long enough, it will appear to move. At first I thought it must be a raven and that it was just standing there on the ice. But as we got closer, I could see that it wasn't. I stopped to allow John and the dogs to catch up. With my monocular I saw, to my amazement, that it was a seal lying on the ice sunning itself. I thought to myself, "This is a tough animal, sun bathing at -35°F." I stalked the seal with my rifle in the hope of giving our dogs some needed fresh meat.

Since I wasn't wearing anything white to camouflage my approach, my chance of succeeding was slim. I did manage to get within 150 yards before I fired. I knew I'd missed when the seal plunged beneath the ice. The sound of my rifle brought the dogs running toward me as if they had just heard the dinner bell. They

should have a rest after every 5 days of travel to mend sore muscles, feet, and paws. To keep our fingers from freezing we swing our arms violently in a windmill motion, letting the centrifugal force push warm blood to the frostbitten tips.

We have been rationing food for the dogs, giving them just enough each day to keep them going. I have figured that with one rest day, we should make it to Siorapaluk with just enough food to feed them the night before we arrive. We will take two rest days sniffed at the scent around the seal's hole, disappointed in me for my miss.

March 27, Rensselaer Bay

Arrived at the hut to find Peter Duneq from Siorapaluk, with two of his relatives from Qeqertat. They were heading north with three teams of dogs to hunt polar bears and had just arrived at the hut the day before. We talked about the route we had just used and laughed together at my and John's misfortunes. They were mainly interested in the terrain that lay ahead for them and if we had spotted any game. Their ears perked up when we mentioned the 10-foot bear we sighted and the seal on the ice.

They'd spent the day hunting ptarmigan and arctic hare in the hills just south of the hut. John and I were glad that their hunt was successful, as they offered us boiled morsels of their meat.

It was pure joy to be back in the warmth of a shelter and able to relax without the constant effort to keep from freezing to death. In the humid 80°F hut, our bodies dripped with sweat. The hut was crowded with the five of us, but John and I welcomed the new faces and conversations in broken English and Inuktut.

March 28

Our Inuit friends left today for the north, and at the end of this first rest day in a while, I cooked dinner for John and me.

I prepared, of all things, Cajun Walrus. After coating the meat heavily with cajun seasoning we'd left behind in bulk on our way north, it fried up nicely in a large pan with butter. Mmmmmm!

Sledding east of Qaanaaq down the Inglefield Bredning Fjord, we follow the eroded sandstone cliffs to Qeqertat.

March 29, -16°F

Deciding to spend an extra day at the hut, today we each took a much-needed bucket bath, the first decent washing in three weeks. Standing in a large pot half full of scummy water, I was naked for the first time in a month. It was a nice feeling to be free of the heavy clothes. We look quite thin and slightly haggard. But, all in all, we feel OK. With bathing, thick layers of calloused, dead skin, the result of frequent frostbite and healing, peeled away from

During a rest break near Siorapaluk, we all enjoy the sun and familiar surroundings.

our fingertips, leaving them pink and tender. The dogs are lying on their sides with big round bellies attached to thin frames—all memories of the past hardship blotted out by two days of "all you can eat."

Aten has crawled into one of our wax-coated depot boxes and is curled up inside, insulated from the snow. He is in heaven, warm and overfed.

For dinner, we are having another first in French cookery—Cajun Pemmican Patties.

We will leave tomorrow.

March 31, Ice Cap

Woke up to a storm that is keeping us from moving. It is just windy enough to obscure the first 5 feet above the surface with blowing snow. It is possible to travel in these conditions, but knowing the possible crevasse dangers ahead, it is better to stay in the safety of our tent.

I am eager to speak with Kelly. She must be worried sick about us as we have been unable to communicate directly since leaving Siorapaluk on February 18.

Around 5:00 p.m. the storm let up and we decided to break camp, pack the sledge, and move out. The dogs are running very well and seem to sense for the first time that we are heading for home. But we're tired and so are the dogs. Sledging across a plateau of ice can be as boring as all get out because it's just flat and white and endless. You can bet the dogs are bored as well. Every now and then the dogs race ahead trying to get to a dog turd left by Peter Duneq's gang some days ago. They stand out like tree trunks on the plateau and are a focal point for the dogs—a cause for excitement.

Finally, we became aware of a slight downhill slope and spotted the cliffs and Nunataks (ice-free mountain tops) that stand as the gate to Clements Markham Glacier. The snow was much more hard-packed this time, and we were in for a fast run. We began to descend rapidly and the sledge overtook the dogs on two occasions. We hurried to put a brake rope over one runner, then added one on the second runner as well. This gave us added control.

After many days of polar night and extreme cold, our dogs enjoy soaking up the warm rays of spring's sun.
Scars like these on Alingnik are caused by fighting for position, which is a characteristic of most Inuit dogs.

Hanging is a centuries-old tradition of dispatching dying dogs. There are many practical reasons for this practice. It reduces the spread of disease because it sheds no blood, and the dogs are high off the ground so other dogs and foxes can't eat from the diseased carcass. The skin is used for clothing, children's fur pants, mittens, or kamik (boot) liners.

We made the downhill run quickly, often clutching a rope and riding the sledge like a rodeo bronco.

The sea coast came into view as we descended to the base of the glacier. On sea ice once again, it was a balmy 31°F. Seeing recent sledge tracks in front of us from several hunters, John and I realized that we were closing a chapter in the story of the expedition. We shook hands at the bottom, satisfied with our achievements over the last month and a half. But underlying our satisfaction was a nagging voice saying that we have failed. Perhaps we should have done this or that. Perhaps we should have taken greater risks and ascended the ice cap in an attempt to reach the Hall Land depot. In the next few days we will have to face our friends who we have let down. Maybe someday we can return and finish what we set out to do.

We arrived at Neqe, a hunting outpost of Siorapaluk, at 2:00 a.m. after traveling 30 miles. There were scraps of walrus fat and meat scattered around the outside of the hut for some 25 yards—the recent signs of a successful hunt. We had difficulty controlling the dogs when we arrived as they were wild to get at the greasy tidbits.

April 1

It was only a 5-hour run from Neqe to Siorapaluk. When we arrived, the community came out to greet us.

We purchased about 90 pounds of walrus meat for our dogs from an elderly man and his wife, who have many sons who are good hunters. Our dogs quickly regained their strength from eating the nutrient-rich meat and from our two-day rest here.

As we walked through the village, we met Peter Duneq's wife, who told us that her husband's hunting party radioed in that they had gotten three bears already and the men are all looking forward to having new polar bear pants.

Later John pointed out some kids playing in our empty supply boxes. The wax-coated cardboard made ideal little sleds, and a group of them were careening down a nearby hill. It seemed that even we were introducing something new and different to the culture.

April 3

About a mile from the village of Qaanaaq, we were confronted with posted bulletins warning of a rabies/distemper outbreak.

As we arrived, we were met by our Danish friends who informed us that about 65 percent of all the dogs in the district had died—a total dead of about 450. Some dogs in the Canadian Arctic had also been infected.

If infected, unvaccinated dogs have little chance of survival. Fortunately, ours were all vaccinated twice before we left Qaanaaq.

*Many local hunters are not as fortunate.
Having been negligent about giving vaccinations,
they have lost some or all of their dogs, and are now
in a state of panic. Their livelihood comes from hunting,
which is impossible without a team of dogs.*

We staked out our dogs in their old location and headed to our quarters where I took the most enjoyable shower of my life! It was the first in a month and a half. Even though I've gone without one for much longer on earlier arctic expeditions, it was never as good as this one. Perhaps I am getting softer as I get older....

April 5, Qaanaaq

Our dog sledge attempt to travel around the northern end of Greenland and continue down the east coast is officially over—for now. John and I have talked it over at great length and both of us are confident that our decision to withdraw was the right one. But we've also been thinking "what if?" With additional reconnaissance and the different ice conditions that another winter would bring, it's possible that it could be done. But that's for another time and another expedition. After all, the most expensive part of our expedition is still in place, our supply depots in the north. Remote and protected from scavenging bears and foxes, they are not going anywhere. In the cold, dry north, the food will last for years—until we can return.

With culture as a main component of the educational program, and both John's and my love for the Inuit people, we've decided to spend the next twenty-two days traveling to the villages and hunting camps that we have not visited thus far. These include Qeqertat, Moriusaq, and Uumannaaq Mountain near Thule Air Base. We hope to document on film and video a style of life that may soon change forever.

April 10, Qeqertat

The village of Qeqertat is 37 miles east of Qaanaaq and home to only nineteen people whose lives are based on the hunting of narwhal during the summer. It is a very isolated and traditional village, with no communal electricity. Water is obtained by melting ice or hauling it from a hole through the ice on a nearby lake. Houses are heated with a small oil stove.

We felt privileged to meet and capture on video Aleqatsiaq Duneq, who is a master at the traditional string figure games called Ajarraaq. Others there, including his nephew Peter Duneq

A passing storm in the village of Qeqertat, a village known for its good narwhal hunting. Population 14.

(unrelated to Peter Duneq from Siorapaluk), also had a few to show. The string figures are learned from elders and have been passed down over the history of their culture. They are usually performed during the dark winter period. It is thought that if the sun sees them, it will bring a cold spring. In the past, most people carried a loop of string about 2 feet in diameter and practiced many different figures. Most of the figures relate to animals or active figures, such as a whale breathing, and a man sliding down an icy slope.

We felt it very important to record Aleqatsiaq's performance, as this is a dying part of the Inuit culture.

Before leaving, Peter decided to join us with his own team of dogs on our sledge trip to Thule Air Base and Moriusaq. The route would include the difficult ascent of the Politiken Brae Glacier, and we were delighted to have the added muscle. Peter is a master dog driver at only eighteen years of age, having started sledging at age nine.

April 17

On our way to Thule, John, Peter, and I set course for a small, snow-covered hut east of the Politiken Brae Glacier. Today was my birthday and we had hopes of using the hut to spend a relatively relaxing evening before tomorrow's difficult ascent of the glacier. When we arrived, there were two teams of dogs already staked next to the hut. As I opened the small door, moist hot air and the smell of wet fur hit my face. I peered inside to see the familiar face of Jens Danielsen smiling at me from the corner where he was operating the Primus stove. "Come in!" he said with a grin.

Aleqatsiaq Duneq from Qeqertat, is a master of Ajarraaq (Inuit string figures), which is a dying art. He can produce 61 string games and figures, such as a fox, caribou, and igloo, from memory.

Approaching Uumannaaq Mountain at the abandoned village of Dundas and Thule Air Base. This was the initial site of the Cape York Inuit until they were relocated to Qaanaaq in the 1950s by the U.S. military. This was also the location of Danish arctic explorers Knud Rasmussen's and Peter Freuchen's North Star Bay Trading Post.

There was little room to "come in" to. The 10-foot-square hut was completely packed with snoring bodies and damp clothing that hung from the ceiling off ropes. Inside were Jens, our friend Mamarut from Herbert Island, and their families. They were also heading to Thule and Moriusaq tomorrow, intending to hunt utoq ("seal-laying-on-the-ice"). I courteously accepted a piece of raw fish from Jens, but declined the invitation to pile into the hut with them. We slept outside in our tent—the same as I have done

on the other three birthdays I have celebrated on expeditions.

April 18

Today the three of us traveled up the Politiken Brae Glacier with Jens and Mamarut. At the bottom of the glacier was a nerve-racking section of dangerous, open water in a swift current coming out from under the glacier. A slim, sloping piece of shoreline just in front of it was our only way to reach the main point of ascent to the glacier. We knew that if a sledge slipped off the bank and into the open water, the current would drag the dogs and possibly the driver under the ice and to their death.

Finally, after much pushing, hauling, barking, and sweating, all sledges, dogs, and families had reached the top. From there it was a steep uphill climb to the summit and a gradual 8-mile descent to the fjord that connected to Thule and Moriusaq.

April 19-20 Thule Air Base

We arrived at the famed Uumannaaq Mountain with its flat and slightly sloping top, an area rich in the history of the Cape York Inuit and Danish explorers like Knud Rasmussen and Peter Freuchen, with their North Star Trading Company. Across North Star Bay lay Thule Air Base, the United States' northernmost installation.

Thule Air Base came into being in 1951 for maintaining an early warning system against possible aggression from Europe, and to provide a supporting airport for long-distance air travel from North America. It was established at Pituffik ("place to keep sledge dogs"). The trading station and existing population were subsequently moved to a new settlement built at Qaanaaq, some 75 miles north.

The base is the home of the 12th Space Warning Squadron and the first Ballistic Missile Early Warning System (BMEWS) designed for the detection and tracking of intercontinental ballistic missiles launched against North America. It also houses one of the 50th Space Wing's satellite remote tracking stations. Numerous large aircraft hangars, service buildings, and flat-topped accommodation buildings greet the visitor, a dramatic contrast to the surrounding arctic landscape!

April 21, Moriusaq

As we approached, the small houses of Moriusaq stuck out like sore thumbs on the empty landscape. These weather-peeled shacks house the village's twenty-five or so residents. We made the rounds, first stopping at Jens Danielsen's parents' house for a welcomed dinner of boiled seal.

We noticed a kayak frame waiting for summer and a new skin covering, along with a newly made sledge and its fresh wood shavings in front of the home of Peter's grandfather. During our brief visit with him, we enjoyed another meal, this time of muskox from a recent hunt, while Peter's grandfather repaired my shortened whip.

I gave him a carton of Prince cigarettes I had purchased on the base, a typical gesture of appreciation for his hospitality.

Peter, having no obligations in his hometown of Qeqertat, opted to spend the rest of the winter here in Moriusaq. A few local girls had their eye on him and I believe this was the deciding

Freeze-dried clothes come off the lines stiff as boards in the village of Moriusaq.

factor to stay, rather than continue with us back to Qaanaaq in the morning.

April 22

Today we ascended the Politiken Brae Glacier from the Moriusaq side. Once we made the summit, we could see all the way down the rest of the glacier, across the fjord and to Qaanaaq, some 16 miles away.

Usaukauq Hensen, grandson of the great polar explorer Matthew Henson, is ascending a moraine field to the west side of the Politiken Brae Glacier on his way to Moriusaq from Qaanaaq.

We saw a team coming up the Qaanaaq side of the glacier through the narrow gully, and I recognized the driver as Usaukauq Henson, the grandson of Matthew Henson, the African-American explorer who accompanied Robert Peary to the North Pole. I watched in admiration as he drove his team, cracking the whip with amazing accuracy, encouraging his dogs to the base of the embankment.

I called to the dogs from above and they slowly made headway in my direction. The sledge was almost to the edge with the dogs still coming as I backed up and called encouragement to them again. Then I realized that the dogs were not coming because I called, but because they wanted to attack, perhaps seeing me as food!

My suspicions were confirmed when one of the leading dogs clamped his jaws around my thickly padded calf. I jerked my leg free and scrambled backward to escape, but found myself up against a sheer rock wall. Just inches away from me, the dogs were commanded to stop as the sledge reached the flat ice of the summit. Usaukauq hurried to me, worried that his dog's teeth might have broken the skin on my leg. Somewhat shaken, I assured him they hadn't—my thick pants and kamiks (boots) had protected me. Then he laughed, thanking me for being bait for his dogs and attracting them up the hill.

Of all the Inuit I have met in the Thule district, I am most fond of this man. If grandfather Matthew Henson was anything like Usaukauq, he was surely one of the main reasons Robert Peary made it to the North Pole.

Now that the descent was clear for us and our dogs, we nervously moved the sledge close to the edge and placed a large brake

Caribou have traditionally been a mainstay for the Inuit, supplying meat and skins for clothing. Today, however,
they are quite scarce in Greenland, but the herds are increasing in the extreme northwest.

In Moriusaq, a kayak frame waits for its summer covering. It hangs on a meat rack above a greasy layer of surplus seal fat.

from my whip. We dug in our heels, dislodging bits of snow that rolled down with us. We all reached the bottom unscathed, only to find the frozen carcass of some poor hunter's dog that hadn't made it.

We negotiated the large rocks and, skirting the open water at the glacier's base, found ourselves back on fjord ice. We were glad and relieved that our glacier travel was over, and somewhat proud of our performance. We arrived back at Qaanaaq from Moriusaq at 3:00 a.m., traveling 50 nautical miles in 13 hours with only two stops for tea breaks.

April 28, Qaanaaq, sold our dogs

John and I said goodbye to our dogs. They had served us well over the past seven months. It was hard giving our furry friends to a new family, but we know they will be well cared for and will live the life for which they were bred.

Mamarut was clearly impressed with the change in Tyson and Holyfield. Over the course of the expedition, they had almost become tame. They had been a hard-working pair throughout and now were clearly an enviable addition to any hunter's team. Mamarut hinted that he would like to buy the pair back, but they were already promised to someone else. Even though they were a horrendous pain at times, we will miss them deeply.

I am very fond of the one named Egileraq, and he will accompany me back to Minnesota in September when I finally head home. Weighing 95 pounds, he is only slightly smaller than Tyson and Holyfield. He has the thickest and longest fur, and rarely caused any fights among the other dogs. He was always cool,

rope over each runner. We then took the dog's traces and ran them underneath the sledge so they came out the back. This would keep the dogs from being run over and injured by the sledge. They would also act as a brake by turning around and digging in their claws if the sledge picked up too much speed, a common method used by the Inuit. John and I pushed the sledge over the edge, John controlling the stanchions while I kept the dogs from running in front of the sledge with discouraging cracks calm, and collected, and should take the flight quite well. Not so with the other dogs. They are still quite wild, and flying would cause them great stress or even death.

I had great difficulty letting go of Aten and would have loved to have brought him back with me to Minnesota. But it would have disheartened him to be separated from his brother Alingnik, so the two of them were returned to their original owner.

Egileraq will be in good company with my other Inuit dogs, making my team in Minnesota an even ten. Someday I hope to breed Egileraq to a female at home named "Libby" after Libby Riddles, the first woman to win the Iditerod sled dog race in Alaska. Kelly and I like to have a few new puppies around our house, plus his addition will help strengthen the bloodlines in my other Inuit dogs.

We had agreed that Torben Diklev should have our sledge as thanks for all of his help over the past months. As John and I pulled it, battered and empty, toward Torben's home, we both fell into a disheartened sadness. We were already missing the dogs.

After traveling more than 1,250 miles by dog sledge, we have finished our campaign in north Greenland. We managed to take some rare photos of north Greenland during the coldest part of the year, an area rarely traveled—almost never in midwinter.

We now head for Ammassalik to gear up for our last leg by kayak to Paamiut.

May 7, flight to Ammassalik

Waiting for the helicopter near a flat piece of ground half a

Tough little Aten reminded me of a scruffy junkyard dog, but he was the friendliest of the bunch; I will miss him a lot.

mile east of Qaanaaq, John and I commented on the dark clouds to the south. We recognized that the once-a-week shuttle to Pituffik 90 miles to the south might not come, due to what looked like a storm brewing. We planned to chopper over to Thule, catch flights to south Greenland, then to east Greenland, then another chopper flight to Ammassalik.

John and I will spend the next two months in Ammassalik

At the base of Granville Fjord, near Moriusaq, John and I pose for a shot, holding the U.S., Greenland, and Australian flags
just a few days before the end of our dog sledge expedition.

training for our kayak journey south, and experiencing part of the short summer with the residents of east Greenland. We will depart by kayak the first week in July when the current and the sun have had a chance to melt and move some of the sea ice blocking our route.

We heard the sound of rotor blades coming from the south and said our final goodbyes to our friends at Qaanaaq.

The pilot was a bit concerned about the approaching weather, but we made it to Thule just before the big blow started. A Storm 3 warning was soon issued, confining everyone indoors. I watched through a small window at the hangar as the wind rocked service trucks parked outside. The near-zero visibility reminded me of those past days stuck in a tent on the Clements Markham Glacier. Looking through the window of a solid and comfortably heated building, it seemed almost impossible that we had survived outside in a similar storm.

The storm left almost as quickly as it had come, and John and I found ourselves seated on a plane at the head of the runway. Gazing out the window to the left of the runway, I noticed the American flag flying briskly at half mast. John said it was in honor of Karl Peary, son of Robert Peary by an Inuit woman, who died today in Qaanaaq at the age of 92.

As we left the ground, I found it coincidental that we were leaving on the same day as Karl. Each of us was off on another adventure, but at the same time marking the end of a chapter in life and exploration.

Now with their new owners, our dogs will surely be as valuable to them as they were to us.

CHAPTER THREE

Kayaking the Icy East Coast

We reached Ammassalik from Qaanaaq in northwest Greenland on May 27. The melt season has begun a month early and, with almost twenty-four hours of light, summer is coming fast. Small arctic flowers are starting to bloom and tundra grasses are turning green. The rivers gush with meltwater from the ice cap and from the heavy snows that accumulated during the winter. The 6,000-foot-high mountains, 2 miles to the north and west, provide an incredible backdrop to the little community. The occasional patch of dark granite can be seen on the south-facing slopes, the remainder still covered by the past winter's snow.

This has given us the opportunity to start training early for our 930-mile kayak journey, which will begin July 9. If we can reach the village of Qaqortoq before the fall storms start in mid-August, we plan to continue on to our original starting point of Paamiut, 180 miles farther up the west coast.

Built on the steep hillsides like most settlements in Greenland, the residents of this village of about 400 are mostly native Greenlanders, while a fourth consider themselves Danish. East Greenlanders, similar to their west coast and northern countrymen in many ways, are also very distinct. Isolated as they are by geography, their language is unrecognizable to those in the west and north. Due to deeper snows and slightly warmer seasons, hunting, fishing, and sledging techniques are also slightly different than elsewhere on the island.

In many ways, the 518 miles of desolate coastline from Ammassalik to south Greenland could be classified as the "Everest of Kayaking." There have been many significant kayak expeditions, but I doubt any were more difficult than ours looked to be.

The outer edges of the eastern coastline are devoid of vegetation and life, except for the occasional sea duck.

May 27 - June 30,

Ammassalik ("place of ammasset")—65°38′North 38°15′West

It is very beautiful here, but at the same time rugged and forbidding. The local Greenlanders are just now starting to go out in their boats to fish and hunt. They cannot travel very far yet due to the pack ice that is still blocking the mouth of the fjord. Later in the summer, when the sea ice starts to melt, they will undertake longer hunting trips by boat for seal, whale, and polar bears. These trips also give them the chance to visit friends and family living in other villages in the district.

Families are netting ammasset (small fish) from the shore, much like the smelt we catch in Lake Superior. They net them by the thousands and dry them on the rocks, to be eaten later, much like fish jerky. They can also fry them in a pan while they are still fresh.

John and I went netting the other day ourselves to supplement our food supply, catching and drying 300 finger-size ammasset for our kayak journey.

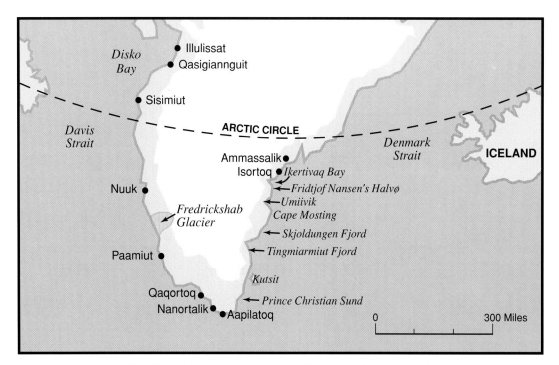

We will travel along much uninhabited coastline, completely self supported,
where no additional supplies can be expected enroute. We must rely on what we can carry in our kayak.

A typical summer morning in Ammassalik begins around 6 a.m. The sun is already beating in through the window because it is light twenty-four hours a day now. There is a chill in the morning air although the sun quickly heats it up as the day progresses—in the summer, temperatures can reach 50°F, bringing small arctic flowers and berries to the fjord valleys.

The sounds of howling huskies also motivate me to get out of bed a little earlier than planned.

The toilet man, who comes three times a week, stops by early to get trash and empty the "honey" bucket. He is sporting the same blue pullover suit worn by all work trades in Greenland.

Many communities have no plumbing or running water. The usual household toilet system is a vented bucket that is emptied by hand when full. Water is gathered either by hand from the nearest freshwater stream, or delivered by the water truck to each home that is equipped with a water storage tank. In the winter, glacial ice is collected from the fjord and put on the home's kerosene heater and melted into drinking water. In settlements like Ammassalik, about 25 percent of the homes have plumbing and flush toilets.

After a quick breakfast of instant coffee and toast and jam, I wander outside to watch the hunters leaving from the harbor, only a few hundred yards from where we are staying. More and more men are going out in their little open boats now that the ice has melted in the fjord, the ammasset are spawning, and the seals are drifting down early with the polar ice.

I notice a lot of activity in the harbor down by the Royal Arctic Line dock. The workers are shifting the large shipping containers,

During summer in Ammassalik, dog sledges are simply left in place from the winter's last run. In the winter, strong piteraq winds, originating from the ice cap, pick up snow in a sandblasting effect, and scour the houses free of paint.

getting ready for the town's first ship of the season. Ammassalik is visited by three ships a year, all during July, with the first one arriving around the second of the month.

These cargo ships come from Denmark, and import what food and materials Greenlanders can't get from the land and sea—products like fuel, building supplies, and miscellaneous hardware. Because of this, living in Greenland is very expensive and the store selections are limited, especially in the smaller communities.

Ammassalik, with its brightly painted buildings, is one of only two settlements on the entire east coast of Greenland. Each community provides a main hub for surrounding smaller villages. Most residents base their livelihood almost entirely on subsistence hunting and fishing. This photo was taken at 3 a.m.

Up from the harbor at the local store, people are already gathered, buying food for that day. Others are people-watching and socializing. The front of the town grocery store seems to be a gathering place in all Greenlandic towns.

Most larger villages have about 5 miles of rough road that connect the airport/heliport and shipyard to the main part of town for the delivery of cargo and mail. The roads also connect to the school, hospital, community office building, store, and post office. Since few individuals own their own vehicles, the roads give access to the town's maintenance vehicles for the removal of snow, garbage, and toilet waste. Most businesses also own a car or truck for errands and work chores.

Many of the villages are built on steep slopes and hills, leaving the only flat spot in town for the heliport. One must truly possess legs of a mountain goat to live here, since walking is the most common form of transportation. The children play and run, unaffected by the steep hills. The adults are also used to the inclines, but the elderly and disabled struggle, as there are few resources to help them with their daily chores.

One morning I watch as Gert Ali, an Inuit elder, departs for a day's hunting. He is outfitted with a small day pack containing his lunch, an extra pair of warm gloves, and shells for the guns. A shotgun and a rifle are slung over one shoulder, a thermos of coffee in one hand, and a pipe filled with Sweet Dublin Tobacco in the other.

Down at the harbor, his umiatsiaq (hunting boat) is anchored away from shore on a 75-foot line attached to a old plastic juice jug that acts as a buoy. The buoy jug is held firm by a line attached to a rock at the bottom of the harbor, and put in a place where the boat can still float during low water. The boats are tied out from shore to

Near the familiar mountain landmarks to the north of Ammassalik, white camouflaged boats used for seal hunting are ready and waiting on the shorefast ice.

prevent them from banging around on the rocks during high and low tides.

A hunter can retrieve his boat from shore by pulling on one side of the continuous circle of rope that is run through a pulley on the buoy. He then pulls the boat next to the dry rock he is standing on and hops in among the hunting and fishing gadgetry.

The usual smell of fish mixed with a dash of boat gas reaches his nostrils. The 16-foot boat's white fiberglass floor is stained with old fish slime and blood from a recent seal. Around the

Rows of torsk (polar cod fish) preserved by drying are a common sight in the villages. Often taken to eat during hunting and fishing excursions, they provide a good source of protein and fat.

plywood completes the standard equipment. The hull of the boat is unintentionally decorated with a variety of different-colored fiberglass patches, mementos of past mishaps negotiating the ice.

For catching polar cod and Arctic char, a small gill net is rolled up in a burlap sack. For the deeper fish, a large spool with monofilament line is secured to the side of the boat with a series of baited hooks a few feet apart. A weight sends this to the bottom of the sea, and it is then rolled back up a few hours later, hopefully, with a few Greenland halibuts or cod on the other end.

A lot of pack ice has come into the fjord due to a south wind and it will take a little longer to get to the hunting and fishing spots. The throttle/steering handle of the outboard motor has been extended with a piece of wood to allow the hunter to sit forward in the boat. This is so he can see better while driving the boat and also to make the boat plane out and handle more smoothly.

The wind created by the swift pace of the boat can change what seemed to be a nice day into a chilly, eye-watering experience. The waves wash up with a "slap" onto the nearby ice pans, and the fresh smell of air after a rain hits the hunter in the face.

Gert's brown eyes scan the water looking for seals as he motors through the water at a fast clip. He is warmly dressed and wearing his bent-up baseball hat to hold down his gray hair. His dark complexion, high cheek bones, and deeply bronzed wrinkles show wisdom and a keen sense of his surroundings. His almost black skin has been tanned by days of hunting, a characteristic of the most active hunters. During the long hours of summer's sunlight, they are often out all day, searching with their binoculars for bears and seals from their little open boats.

inside of the boat, are stored long-handled tools: an ice chisel, an ammasset scoop net, and a long broom handle with a very large fish hook attached to the end by two hose clamps. This is one of the hunter's main tools. It is used to gaff shot seals, big fish, or boat ropes, or just to hold the boat next to the ice edge.

A small, lid-free plywood box sits in the middle of the boat and houses the Primus kerosene stove. The plywood box blocks the wind from the stove's burner and cook pot. It also seconds as a table, seat, or mini work bench. A makeshift windshield of

Dwarfed by ice pans, a family wiggles their small boat through the ice on their way to summer camp.
The summer camps are located near areas of good berry picking, seal hunting, and ammasset and arctic char netting.

Discipline and Education

Shy boys from Ammassalik.

Greenlandic children are raised fairly unrestricted. They are only stopped from doing something if it is physically harmful to them or another. No time schedule is put on the kids. They can play, go to bed, and eat when they feel like it. It is believed by the Inuit that this complete freedom gives the children better understanding and confidence in life as they grow up.

Another custom is practiced while growing up: if, for example, a child is playing with some others on the rocks and falls down and lands in the dirt, all the other children and even the adults will point at the child and laugh. The child will usually pick himself or herself up and, with a frown of pride, brush off the dirt and carry on with the play. This unusual technique is to make the children learn from their mistakes. It is also intended to teach that it is important to laugh at oneself.

School children in Greenland make up a great proportion of the population. Many families have five or six children, a much higher number than in western Europe. Little education in the traditional hunting and subsistence methods, used by the Inuit for thousands of years, is given at schools. These skills must be passed on by parents or older relatives still active in these methods. The students are taught at school, until at least grade 9, primarily by Danish teachers promoting academic education in line with accepted European standards.

The schools in the small settlements have limited resources, and sometimes there are no formally trained teachers. Many children miss lessons and parts of the school year due to lengthy hunting and fishing excursions.

At grade levels 10 and 11, students can either choose an expanded academic curriculum or a basic curriculum, with classes held both in Greenland and in Denmark. The quality of schooling in Denmark is still superior to the Greenlandic standard, but the Greenlandic system is slowly catching up. Once students obtain the high school diploma, they can be accepted into further university studies in Denmark or trade schools in Greenland and Denmark. An increasing number of students are pursuing higher education in order to gain administrative and professional jobs in Greenland.

Seals

Seal is hunted by all, and every part of the animal is used. The meat supplies a nutritious source of protein and fat to keep the people warm. The skin is used for making clothing. The seal is usually dressed by taking the meat and either putting it on the stove for a meal or hanging it on the meat rack to dry for later use. The liver and small intestine are kept to be eaten and the remaining entrails are fed to the dogs.

The skin is then scraped free of fat with an ulu, a moon-shaped blade attached to a palm handle made of wood, bone, or ivory. The butcher's hands become shiny with grease as the fat rolls off the hide with each cut. It is scraped down to the white leather. The hide is then washed and stretched on a frame, then dried outside. Seal skin is mainly used in making kamiks, pants, and mittens.

There are basically three ways to preserve the meat. The most common is simply to cut the meat into thin strips and hang it outside to dry. The second is to store the dried meat (or fish) in seal oil. Sometimes edible plants and berries are put in the oil as well to help keep them preserved. The third method of preservation is to bury the meat in the skin under rocks away from the sun in the summer, and let the fat soak deep into the meat which marblizes it. Months later it is dug up and eaten, when it has become fermented and considered a delicacy.

An elder man from Ammassalik waterproofs the seams of an umiaq (woman's boat) with rendered seal fat. Umiaqs are made from bearded seal or walrus skin. In the background, a traditional hut made of stone and sod, which were once used throughout Greenland.

It was never easy finding a suitable and flat sight for making camp. We also had difficulties finding places to anchor the tent and kayak from potential winds.

It is 9 a.m. Gert is already returning from his early morning hunt. As I give him a hand pulling in his boat, I see he's been successful. He's got eight seals draped across the hood and rear of his boat. Their heads show the fatal wounds as they dangle to the water so no blood gets in the boat.

It's low tide, and the hunter throws me the line to his boat and I drag it to the landing through the sand a few inches below the water. He then passes me the seals, which I stake at the top of the ramp. This ramp is used by most hunters to bring in their catch. It is close to the hunters market, which is a small open-air structure with a table for placing the catch of the day. Hunters gather around throughout the day, smoking their pipes and telling stories of the day's hunt. Most are outfitted in the black and gray rubber knee boots that can be bought at the hardware counter of the local store.

On the table inside are ducks, sea weed, dried ammassets, and pieces of cut-up seal ready for the pot. The hunters sell some of their catch so they can purchase boat gas, repairs, and hunting supplies. Most hunters also have meat racks at their homes to dry extra seal meat and fish for use come winter.

July 3

Gert tells us that he has never seen this much "big ice" from the Arctic Ocean choking the water this late in the summer. He has heard that the icebreaker, which supplies the village three times a year, will not arrive today because it is caught in the ice 10 miles offshore. Because of this year's warm winter and early summer, more ice is being released from the Arctic Ocean and glaciers—drifting down toward us. We will have our work cut out for us trying to paddle in all of this.

The many difficulties of negotiating the moving pack ice, the weather, and the limited number of places to land safely on shore will prove to be tiring for us. We know the cards are stacked against us. We will have to rely on our preparations, experience, and determination to get us through.

July 9

It was a crisp morning when we left Ammassalik at 6:30 a.m. in our tandem kayak, skimming through a thin layer of ice that had formed in the harbor overnight. Loaded with 175 pounds of food, fuel, and equipment, we half wondered if the heavy craft would sink or float when we placed it in the water. We need this large amount of supplies to carry us through the uninhabited coastline we are about to tackle. There is no place to resupply along the way and we have placed no depots along our route.

July 10, Isortoq ("unclear water")

The big tides and current have kept the pack ice out from the rocky shore and cliff face a few yards, allowing us a narrow but negotiable passage. We passed the last pocket of habitation, the small village of Isortoq. There is little or no vegetation south of this point to support life. Only the vast ice cap and coal-black mountains provide a backdrop to this coastal hunting area.

At night we hear the thundering of calving icebergs in the distance, reminding us of our experiences on the west coast and of the dangers that surely lie ahead.

From this scouting vantage point looking south, I wondered how we would continue.

We had to climb hills several times a day to look for a route through the impervious ice. I often used a monocular and jotted down a potential passage.

July 11

Frustrated, we have been stopped by the ice. We climbed a nearby hill to get a better view and looked out at an endless sheet of compressed, floating ice pack for as far as we could see. It seemed utterly impossible to complete the task before us tomorrow and perhaps in the days ahead.

Disheartened, I thought, "Who are we to challenge this?"

July 12

Overnight the ice ahead slacked a bit and we were able to wiggle our way across Ikertivaq Bay between the floes of ice. With barely enough water between the floes to float the kayak, our paddles were uselessly hitting the ice. We had to resort to the use of our homemade gaff hooks, reaching forward from our cockpits and grabbing the ice in rhythm to pull ourselves along. Many times we kayaked by huge pieces of ice that would roll over just after we passed through. There weren't a lot of choices. Either we kept going or we turned around—and we didn't consider that an option. Progress was slow. We detoured about half of the time as we zigzagged south. We fought our way forward and, exhausted after 9½ hours, we stopped 1½ hours early to camp.

July 13

Our camp this evening was located near a centuries old, Inuit stone grave. It was an eerie sight, the skull of the grave's occupant visible through the rocks, illuminated by a bright orange, three-quarter moon rising over an iceberg. Traveling by kayak like the Inuit who were here centuries ago, gave us insight and the gift of

Camping on rock meant anchoring the tent to the kayak and then tying a knot in the kayak bow line that could be wedged in a crack in the rock.

With leads too wide to jump over, we used our kayaks as a bridge. I would stabilize one end so John could cross, then he would do the same for me.

thinking like them. We instinctively take the best and safest way south through passages and backwaters of limited ice. In this way we often come across hidden Inuit encampments, some not marked on our detailed maps. These hard-to-find places were apparently hidden from past anthropological expeditions by helicopter and ship. I am reminded of another ancient Inuit encampment, one we discovered during our winter of dog sledging. On that occasion—hungry, darkness setting in, and the temperature at -45°F—I had stood in one of seven stone tent rings and was

amazed at the difficult life the early Inuit must have led. I have boundless respect and a sense of awe for what they had to endure. I have a similar feeling of admiration and respect here on the east coast, more than a hundred miles from anything resembling civilization as I know it.

July 14

John and I spent half the day manhauling our kayak over dangerous shifting ice and the other half paddling through thick brash ice—the small ice shards created when icebergs calving from an active glacier hit the water and splinter. We put makeshift rope harnesses over our shoulders and pulled our kayaks across the pans of ice. We often found ourselves plunged up to our waist in the icy water when a piece of rotten ice suddenly broke beneath our feet. Scrambling to get out, we could feel the cold water against the outside of our dry suits, chilling us. But we were able to make some progress.

We seemed so insignificant, surrounded by the towering icebergs as we fought our way to safer ground. Pieces of these immense bergs were breaking off all around and falling to the water, causing waves that swamped the ice floes near us. Agreeing that we were grossly pushing our luck and safety margin, we expended what energy we had left to made a quick landfall.

July 16

We had decent paddling most of the day and then our luck ran out when a sudden wind came up. To be caught in the middle of a fjord with the onset of a piteraq wind would have meant

One of our biggest fears was taking an unintentional dip in the icy water. High on our priority list was avoiding that mishap at all cost.

Last winter's snows are still prevalent on hillsides on this evening in July.

injury or death, so the decision was made to retreat about 3 miles to the nearest shore where we waited about an hour until the weather improved.

I think it's because we are always slightly afraid that we are still alive. It's when you have no fear that you become reckless.

Halfway across we were again using our paddles as pushpoles against the ice. By pushing simultaneously, we inched forward half a boat length at a time. The paddles are taking a beating, but are still functional. We are starting to look for a storm day to give us an excuse to lay over and rest our very overworked muscles.

We finished up the day near Fridtjof Nansen's Halvø (half-island, or peninsula). This is an ice-capped peninsula that juts out into the Denmark Strait and is named after the famous Norwegian explorer, Fridtjof Nansen. He used this area as a departure point for his famous first crossing of Greenland's ice cap in 1888.

July 17, Umiivik Area

268 miles down, and only 250 miles to go before reaching habitation again.

We camped 200 yards from a very active glacier, which awakened us each time it calved a berg. This happened three times last night. Each time, John and I both jumped up, half asleep, to look through the tent flap, praying to see that our kayak had not been washed away, leaving us here to starve to death.

We overslept for the fourth time this morning. We have been pushing our physical limits for several days now and it's understandable why we cannot budge from our sleeping bags. But in spite of our fatigue, this is unacceptable. We must remedy the

Icebergs and sea ice slowly drift south along the east coast, melting along the way, around the southern tip and then north along the west coast.

John, grabbing a piece of brash ice with his paddle, moves slowly though the "gruel" near Cape Mosting. Our paddles and kayak were taking much abuse from the ice.

problem if we don't want to run out of food before reaching supplies in the distant south.

It is John's responsibility during this leg of the expedition to get up in the mornings and prepare the usual oatmeal and mug of hot coffee. This allows me an additional 30 minutes of rest in the mornings. John gets his extra minutes in the evening by hitting the hay early. It was my job on the dog sledge journey to be the "morning person" and I can readily understand the occasional, unintentional, sleep-in.

Weather permitting, we sleep without a tent and I keep a safe distance from John's snoring and the alarm clock. This morning, I questioned John as to why he thought we were late again in getting up. As he removed his foam ear plugs, he grumbled that he never heard a peep from the clock and thought maybe it was broken. I immediately realized the ear plugs and exhaustion were the source of our problem!

This persuaded me that we truly did need more rest so we adjusted our schedule to allow another 30 minutes in the morning, and John slept with the alarm clock inches from his head.

July 19

We finally made camp on the south side of Cape Mosting after 9 hours of pushpoling. Jutting out farther into the sea than the rest of the shoreline, this landform produces dangerous currents at its base. With only 3 feet of open water between the ice and the cape's sheer granite wall, we had to be very alert, keeping an eye on the ice so as not to get crushed against the rock wall to our right. Huge, unstoppable chunks of fast-moving ice really put the fear in John and me as they ground away at each other, passing us at a fast 4 mph clip.

The only consolation for today's hard work was the fact that we saw some green vegetation in the form of a vine carpet of 2-inch-tall blackberry bushes and moss. What a sight after days of bare rock and ice!

July 20

There was a high north wind this morning, so we decided to use our small sail for the first time. First, we mounted the 2-foot inflatable pontoons to the sides of the kayak to keep it from tipping in the choppy water or from a sudden gust of wind. The fast, but brief, 2-hour sail had us using the rudder to dodge ice chunks. Our sailing ended when we were confronted by an impassable sheet of ice, so we gaff-hooked and manhauled our way across South Skoldungen Fjord, making only 6 miles in 7 hours. We even used our 18-foot kayak as a bridge to span two pans of ice separated by open water too wide to jump.

How many days can we keep on dragging and dragging our heavy kayak over the awful, shifting ice before our bodies give out? Before time and food run out? If we are late in getting to south Greenland, the fall storms will put an end to the expedition. In order to reach south Greenland and safety at Prince Christian Sund weather station, we need to maintain our daily routine of 11 hours paddling, 9 hours for sleep, and 4 hours for camp duties.

July 23

We are amazed at the abuse our Werner composite paddles are

Sometimes the shapes of small icebergs were a virtual piece of art, such as this one in Prince Christian Sund near Aapilatoq.

taking. They are being used as ice chisels, pry bars, and pushpoles and still remain functional as paddles.

Tension is high and we argue about stupid things like the proper and most efficient way to paddle. You would think after last season's kayaking we would have that down pat. At a rest and lunch break, we looked over a map discussing the possibility of taking a long detour through an inside passage in the hope of avoiding the horrendous ice.

Cod liver oil and aspirin are now part of our evening rations.

We waited in a protected bay for the wind to die down up ahead. Cigar-shaped clouds indicate strong piteraq winds to the south, funneled down a fjord from the ice cap.

They help relieve the fatigue of our muscles and joints so we can sleep. Body maintenance chores consist of applying Tiger Balm each morning to sore areas followed by a series of stretching exercises. We are badly in need of a day of rest to repair torn muscles and heal joints, but we can only afford to have a rest day if we are stopped by a storm.

July 24

Because we decided to take a chance on an inland channel route we were able to paddle all day without having to deal with ice, and made a remarkable 25 miles. We are starting to see more and more driftwood and logs as we travel south.

Today we have entered the Tingmiarmiut Fjord system, which cuts deep into one of the thickest parts of Greenland's inland ice cap. We have to be on alert for the piteraq winds, which are well known in this area. The wind can reach speeds of 200 mph as it descends from the ice cap and funnels through the fjord and out to sea. Cigar-shaped clouds above mountain tops are warning signs for us to stay put.

July 25

We quit 1½ hours early today, exhausted from paddling into a headwind. As it is, we both started out this morning shy on sleep. All last night, the bursting and rolling of bergs kept us awake. We could have slept with earplugs, but then we wouldn't know if a polar bear was in camp until he was dragging one of us out of the tent . . .

The heat of the 24 hours of sun melted the bergs at an incredible rate. Besides the water dripping from the sides,
huge bergs formed interior lakes with rivers of melt water flowing off them.

Narrow fjords with mile-high sheer rock faces down to the waterline made us feel small and insignificant.

July 28

It rained all day. The damp and cold magnified our stiff joints and sore muscles after a record 28-mile day. John's aching right shoulder gave him so much pain that he actually said something about it. For him to complain is rare, so it tells me that our condition is bad. The throbbing of our joints at night keeps us from a decent night's sleep. I shot two gullimiuts—small, black-and-white sea ducks that feed on shrimp and small fish—in the hope that the fresh meat and protein will help repair our torn muscles.

July 30—60°33′ North 42°50′ West

We have been twenty-two days without radio contact and are eager to let our families know we are OK. At last, from Kutsit, a small island just a mile off the coast, we made contact through an isolated VHF repeater 52 miles to the south to Qaqortoq Radio Station on the west coast of Greenland.

The man working the radio at the time couldn't believe we were transmitting from the east coast, a first for him. The communication experts said we wouldn't be able to transmit beyond a maximum range of 30 miles. We shouldn't have gotten any reception for another 22 miles. The radio station relayed a message to Kelly in Minnesota that we are OK.

Now that we can make radio contact in case of emergency, I know we have passed a critical point in the expedition. This has taken a huge load off our shoulders. Not a day went by that I didn't think we could lose our lives out here. We have also increased our safety margin by being able to call for weather forecasts.

I renamed this special rocky island "Jacob Island," after my son, Jacob. We built a three-foot stone cairn on its summit, the only cairn we erected during the entire 1½-year expedition. In it we placed a note in honor of my son and our project.

August 3

Today at 8:30 a.m. we reached the manned weather station at Prince Christian Sund in dense fog, navigating by the sound of its generator, and surprising the six Danes stationed there. The "station" was a handful of antenna-sprouting, green shacks anchored to bedrock with cables over the roofs to keep the buildings from blowing off the escarpment. From the water's edge we climbed long flights of wooden stairs to the summit and startled the station chief who emerged from the stations entrance as we approached. Completely unexpecting of visitors, he responded to our English greeting of "hello" with a commanding voice, demanding in English to know who we were and what we were doing there! After a short chat he gave us a big smile and an inviting "You must be hungry." Thoughts of open-faced Danish sandwiches ran through our heads as he introduced us to the rest of the crew. All the men were casually clothed for the comfort of their little huts, and aged from 30 to 45, sporting well-fed midsections. They were astounded that we had just kayaked the 518 miles of treacherous coastline from Ammassalik in 26 days. Not having much company in those parts, they greeted us with open arms and a fine Danish meal prepared by the cook. We left with full bellies, newly acquired knowledge of the route ahead, and warm farewells from the men.

The weather station is located here for a good reason—the weather is absolutely foul most of the time. It is like Cape Horn at the southern tip of South America where many weather and ocean conditions converge to produce chaotic seas and heavy winds. These, combined with unpredictable winds off the ice cap, create the most difficult shipping and flying conditions in the Northern Hemisphere.

August 4

We left the station paddling west, only to be stopped after 9 miles by a headwind that funneled down the sheer sides of the fjord. The mosquitoes and gnats are out. They drove us nuts while

Out of nowhere, icebergs would lift out of the fog. Due to ice and unfavorable winds, we were only able to use our compact sail a total of two hours on the entire east coast journey.

The changing currents and tides along Prince Christian Sund made timing our paddling stokes crucial.

we set up our tent. These little arctic chewers are bad—maybe worse than those in the Minnesota northwoods during the month of June. Thank goodness that the bug season in the Arctic is short and usually only lasts a few hours during the warmth of the day.

Prince Christian Sund is a narrow, current-driven waterway slicing through 5,000-foot peaks. The 40-mile sound connects Greenland's east and west coasts and offers a safer alternative to navigating the turbulent waters of Cape Farvel, the island's southernmost tip.

August 6

We cannot travel again today due to a 30 mph west wind. We filled the time collecting small blackberries and mushrooms to supplement our food supply. Tent time is spent writing in our journals and reading the only two books we brought—*Learning to Speak Danish* and the Bible.

Staying put for the last three days has seemed like an eternity compared to our nonstop going a few days ago. The only good coming from it is that our joints and muscles are finally getting some deserved rest.

August 10

We reached Aapilatoq today—59°59′North 44°35′West—553 miles since leaving from Ammassalik. There are 427 miles remaining to our goal of Paamiut. Aapilatoq is, in my judgment, the most beautiful of all the villages we visited in Greenland. The settlement of forty or so inhabitants sits on a small island, 100 yards offshore. This is the only location you could even begin to consider flat. From the shoreline, mountains rise up 6,000 feet to create a megalithic amphitheater, the small red, yellow, and blue houses of Aapilatoq sitting at center stage. Unfortunately, the scenery is obscured most of the time by clouds and rain.

It was nice to be in a village again, with the sight of hunting boats coming and going, and people in rubber boots, busy getting outside work done before the short breath of summer was over. An elderly man and his wife met us on the beach and asked us in Greenlandic and broken English where we had come from. We told him "Ammassalik—32 days!" With big eyes he repeated "Ammassalik?" as he pointed with his finger behind him up the coast and over the ice cap.

The word got out that newcomers had arrived and within an hour, we had intermingled with most of the curious kids and older folks. Others, dressed in tattered wool sweaters and cotton anoraks, middle-aged and busy with chores, came by intermittently to offer nods from a distance or to introduce themselves as they looked over our kayak and its design.

We snacked on some dried fish with several kids who played in our beached kayak, acting out paddling motions and digging through the hatches.

We sat down on a wooden bench next to six residents having a relaxing smoke on the sunny side of a small boat house, protected from a stiff wind. All were laughing at the funny language coming out of our mouths as we tried to explain our journey in the rough mixture of Greenlandic and Danish that we had learned. Later, we were taken by an older man, retired from younger hunting days, to his house where his wife showed us old

Hunting boats are often forced to wiggle through the narrow gaps in the ice. They are able to push smaller chunks out of the way with the bow.

sepia-colored family photographs that decorated the walls while she fed us wonderful tea and homemade cakes. We learned from local hunters that ice conditions there were as bad as could be remembered, making it difficult to hunt seal and net fish. The first supply ship of the year, scheduled for May, had just arrived a week ago. Now the foul weather brought on by autumn was beginning to cast doubt on the possibility of reaching Paamiut. John and I were loath to consider stopping short of our final goal,

Gales like this one frequent Greenland's south end. They come suddenly, leaving unwary kayakers fighting for their lives.

sides by mile-high, sheer granite cliffs. These walls rise vertically from the water's edge and create some of the highest vertical drops in the world. It's a rock climber's dream come true and I developed a stiff neck looking up. For some reason, the silhouetted peaks and the stars reminded me of home as we kayaked by. We stopped at 11:00 p.m. and will sleep directly on the rocks tonight, too tired to bother with the tent.

August 12

A gale broke out this morning and the intense wind is grabbing sheets of water off the sea and spraying the tent. Luckily, we set the tent up last night in a niche in the rock wall, so we are protected from the wind. At one point, we seemed to be in the eye of the storm. A lone opening of clear sky was overhead and the sun's brief appearance put light on Mother Nature's wrath at sea. The water was in total chaos, churning and agitating as if in an immense washing machine. The icebergs offshore were swaying back and forth, dancing to the rhythmic swell of the sea.

A storm after the gale has made western progress toward the village of Nanortalik impossibly slow and dangerous. We have made only 5 miles in the last four days. The weather, more severe than normal for August, has delayed us. We have paddled only four out of the last thirteen days. It is not looking good for our final leg from Qaqortoq to Paamiut.

We passed the time in our sleeping bags, listening and waiting for the wind to abate. The alarm clock gets us up every six hours to check on the weather, but always with the same bad news.

but we also recognized the increased risk that pushing on might entail.

We left Aapilatoq at 7:00 p.m. that same day when the wind died down toward evening. We preferred not to paddle in the dark, but the wind had kept us from making much progress in the past days.

We continued on down the narrow fjord, with a three-quarter moon and Venus lighting our way. The fjord is flanked on both

August 13

It's John's birthday today, the second one on this expedition, and for a treat I made us a birthday dinner of hand-picked mushroom soup.

August 15

We had the pleasure of seeing many fin whales during the 15 miles to Nanortalik. It was nice compensation for the past gloomy days.

We have reluctantly decided that the expedition will end at Qaqortoq instead of Paamiut. The weather has become increasingly severe and unpredictable, and our gut feel is that attempting it would be a bad choice. Over the last fifteen months, our instincts have kept us alive, so we'll follow them one more time.

We wonder about Lone Madsen, a Danish kayaker we met in Ammassalik. She's a stocky, middle-aged woman with a degree in photo journalism. She contains the very *spirit* of adventure, which led her to move from Denmark in 1992 to live in the small Greenlandic village of Kangaatsiaq. There she raised sledge dogs, wrote about her experiences, and organized significant dog sledge and kayak journeys on the west coast, along with a 300-mile crossing of Greenland's ice cap. She was scheduled to depart from Ammassalik on August 1 and follow our course south.

August 18

We left Nanortalik bound for the village of Qaqortoq. The mornings have been getting colder as fall approaches. The abundant blackberries are receiving their final picking by the local

There were days when the wind brought the pack ice in tight to shore; somehow, we managed to get through what seemed impossible.

Luckily, during the expedition, we were never forced to completely submerge in our dry suits. So we decided to christen them and toast our sponsors, supporters, and friends!

women. The tundra is starting to show faint signs of rust color that indicate the onset of autumn.

The weather has been anything but stable, with strong winds bringing in the change of seasons. Waterfowl can be seen massing for their journey south. A thick fog has obscured our route during the morning hours and for the first time we are forced to paddle by compass and GPS. We made 20 miles today and are exhausted.

Shortly before heading to a piece of shoreline suitable for a

camp spot, we ran into a pod of four whales. They were fin whales feeding on small shrimp that had concentrated between a large drifting iceberg and the shore. The whales swam almost directly under our kayak, boiling the water with their enormous fins as they worked together to round up the shrimp. Once they had a dense number of these crustaceans encircled, they would take turns surfacing in the middle, their huge mouths gaping to the sky. It was wonderfully rewarding to see these kings of the ocean.

August 20

We have only 15.5 miles to paddle before we reach Qaqortoq and the end of the expedition. It is so hard for me to believe that it will soon be over.

Both physically and mentally, this has been a steady drain on me—fighting a web of logistical problems, fatigue, and loneliness—and depression—from long bouts of isolation and difficult conditions. This is not surprising when you consider during the last 15 months John and I have spent 150 days in the confines of a tent. John seems to be faring slightly better, perhaps from his past extended stints in Antarctica.

I have tried not to focus on the finish line until now. Had I done this early in the project, the enormous task in front of us would have seemed impossible to achieve. We took one day at a time, made this expedition our lives, and never looked too far ahead.

A lot of thoughts are running through my head now, knowing that we are only hours from finishing—my wife, friends, family, trees, green grass, past days working on the expedition, sledging in Qaanaaq—a whole collage of images. After three years of nothing else but Greenland, I will be free of the commitment which has given me knowledge, hardship, and rewards far beyond my expectations. How nice it will be to go home.

Qaqortoq—the finish!

Today was our last day. All in all, we traveled 3,200 miles during this odyssey. We entered the small bay into Qaqortoq after paddling 750 miles from Ammassalik in 43 days.

Although I had an ear-to-ear smile on my face when we stepped onto the shore of the settlement, I was somehow expecting to be happier. Perhaps even crying out that we had finally made it, ecstatic with accomplishment. But there was none of that. Just a smile and quiet contemplation.

We had adapted to our surroundings quite well. Emotionally, maybe better than we had ever anticipated. We had forced ourselves to curb our thoughts and to contain our emotions over the last fifteen months. It was the only way we could cope with the mammoth task before us each day. I realized then that I couldn't just turn my emotions on like a faucet and let them flow again. It would take some time. Perhaps one day in the near future, it will sink in, hitting both of us like a ton of bricks. Then the emotions will flow from thoughts of what we have accomplished.

For now, the pop of a champagne cork punctuates a bittersweet ending.

The sculpted beauty of Greenland's ice is something John and I will never forget. At times, it seemed to have a life of its own, drifting, calving, and rolling over. Greenland truly is where ice is born.

AFTERWORD

At home in Minnesota, the warm September left over from El Niño offered the first real summer-like weather I've enjoyed in two years. While in Greenland, John and I often talked about spending time on the warm beaches of Australia after the expedition was over, but those Minnesota autumn days were perfectly fine for me. I marveled at the bright greens of the grass and leaves. Oh, yes—and trees. I love those trees!

During the four-day trip back to Minnesota and the months that followed, I have had the chance to reflect on what we achieved during the course of our fifteen-month expedition. I have to say I feel it's aged me far more than that. Even more from the frustrating and mentally draining months spent in preparation than from the expedition itself.

Foremost, I am grateful that both John and I are still alive after such a trek. Perhaps this is the ultimate reward for careful planning and discretion. Shortly after getting back to Minnesota, the enormous physical risk that our journey presented hit home when I received a sobering e-mail message from the Danish Polar Center. The message indicated that Lone Madsen, an accomplished Danish kayaker and journalist, had died attempting to follow the same eastern coastal route we had just finished.

During our preparations, experienced arctic travelers from Denmark and the United States were openly skeptical of our chances and even our sanity, flatly stating that our expedition journeys by kayak were impossible to achieve. In the end, we believed in ourselves and succeeded. And I cannot imagine a better way to see Greenland and all that it is, mile by mile, than from kayak and dog sledge.

Part of our success was attributed to being able to communicate with each other about weather, route, or our feelings—things you can't always do in separate kayaks.

We pulled the kayak over sea ice off and on for most of the journey. It was exhausting work dragging the kayak over hidden leads and soft snow in drysuits.

After returning home I found it hard to focus and adjust to the routines of modern life. After being gone for so long, I felt reserved in the company of friends and slightly depressed. I had to get my mind back in its old rhythm again with a whole different way of thinking—paying bills, talking on the phone, driving a vehicle, going to the grocery store. During the last year and a half my focus had been on the Greenland journey. I had been on that same path for a long time, and when it finally came to an end, I needed time to regroup and assess the things that we had just accomplished before I could carry on with a new vision. This transition time lasted about five months. In 1992, after traveling by dog team on a 3,000-mile, eight-month journey across the Arctic's famed Northwest Passage, it had taken me about three months to get my energy and drive back, so I guess I've found my inner recuperation pace.

I've already forgotten the hardships and instead reflect on the simplicity of our existance "out there" and the natural surroundings of a long and difficult journey that allowed me time to be alone, a chance to escape the stimulations of everyday life and organize my thoughts without distractions. I reflect on the important things in life and the purpose of our presence here on earth. Some think I am crazy for wanting to go back.

When life seems to be going good, one forgets the simple, important things in life. But when hardship and struggle are present, the importance of the simple things in life shines through.

John stayed in Minnesota for a few weeks before continuing on to his home in Queensland, Australia. His departure was an emotional one for both of us. Saying "goodbye" after having been through so much together was harder than either of us expected.

Even with the camera's autofocus system frozen—at -57°F in Kane Basin—this photo tells a great story.

The last 15 months have brought John and I a sense of accomplishment, and gratefulness toward the Greenlandic people. Even through the tears of frustration and disappointment of failure, we know we will be back to reach our ultimate goal of circumnavigating the island.

After spending some time relaxing and getting reacquainted with "normal" life, he was off again, this time back to Antarctica for another stint with the Australian National Antarctic Research Expedition as an electrical project officer. His main responsibilities there deal with energy management and generating power from renewable resources. He's talked of eventually starting a company that focuses on renewable energy sources such as wind and sun. He says he often thinks about the skills he learned during his time in Greenland and finds himself wondering if the modern world really has to be so complicated, cluttered, and artificially stimulating.

As I've been preparing material for this book, John has offered me some of his own thoughts and reflections:

"Strange as it seems, on the journey it may have taken us a whole day or more to cover the same distance many commuters cover in one hour going to work or school. But we chose to do this. Not for punishment, but to experience Greenland the way that it has been experienced for centuries.

"We endured the hardships of the weather, the frightening waves pounding our fragile craft in frigid waters, the disappointment of having our passage blocked by ice, and the isolation—just the two of us, miniscule in the grandness of the landscape. Remembering the excitement of watching whales breach, the colors of the twilight sky, and the friendship with our dogs and with each other fills me with an immense inner sense of pride and joy. I will forever treasure my lasting impressions of the joyful and proud Inuit who never failed to make us feel welcome and always bid us farewell with advice and good wishes."

John finished up his program at Davis Base, Antarctica, and sent me email while traveling home onboard the icebreaker *Aurora Australis*. He described his experience of watching enormous elephant seals as they squeezed together reluctantly, then burped and snored their days away while their skin molted off. He also shared with me his plan to purchase a camper van and to tour Australia's outback for a while. He's not one to let grass grow under his feet.

Both John and I knew at the time that it was not the end of our dream to circumnavigate the island. With luck, we will go back someday to finish what we set out to do!

While we were gone, Princess Diana was killed, embassies were bombed in Africa, two hurricanes named George and Mitch killed thousands of people in South America and the Caribbean, and Mother Teresa died. Although what we did is miniscule when compared to things that affected so many on a world scale, John and I are proud that our efforts contributed to knowledge of a little-known part of our world and the people who live there. We are also hopeful that we instilled courage into those fearful of taking the first step toward making their own dream a reality.

ACKNOWLEDGMENTS

From the very conception of this expedition in the spring of 1995 to the finish 3½ years later, a multitude of gracious individuals came to our aid in making this dream come true.

I first want to thank my wife, Kelly, who held the fort during all those days of me being gone on expeditions. The long nights spent wondering if I were alive or dead and the goodbyes that never get any easier. Her talents were essential to the successful outcome of the expedition and this book. For the expedition she had written and developed the concurrent educational curriculum along with Eric Robertson and Rod Haenke of Learning Outfitters, Inc., in St. Paul, Minnesota. Together they developed a nationwide program, utilizing both the curriculum, computer, and Internet as educational tools.

Schoolchildren could follow the team's progress on the expedition's web site, interacting with the team through questions and answers on the trail. For this book, Kelly has complemented that program wonderfully with her linoleum-cut prints, which helped me bring forth the true spirit of its contents. She has allowed me to follow my dreams, for which I am truly grateful.

I would like to thank John Hoelscher for giving 2½ years of his life to this project, which never would have been possible without him. We endured appalling conditions, about which John never complained. Our trials together created an interwoven bond of friendship that cannot easily be broken. I would like to thank John for his reflections and insights from Greenland, which helped me in the writing of this book.

John cleaned a sea duck I shot to supplement our dwindling food supplies. The active glacier in the background calved three icebergs during the night. We were not looking forward to having to travel near these unstable and moving pieces on our way south.

In northern Minnesota with my sled dog Slava.

A big "bear hug" goes out to my good friend Gary Atwood, who was there from the beginning. He spent many days editing my diary, which really consisted of a 50,000-word sentence, and contributed his ability to clearly state what I was feeling. He also acted as office manager to the expedition, in the early stages helping with the mammoth task of expedition logistics, fund-raising, and letter writing. He gave our office an added touch of professionalism in an otherwise chaotic-looking situation.

I extend my appreciation to Barbara Harold at Creative Publishing International/Northword Press for her editing, insight, and encouragement needed to fulfill this dream.

A special thanks goes to our two Lead Sponsors, for without their faith in our project we never would have been able to make the first step: Jerry Rinder with Swiss Army Brands and the Victorinox-Swiss Army Knife, which, for over ten years, has always been included on my expedition checklists as an essential item; and Greg Frisby and Doug McCrossen with Frisby Technologies for the ComforTemp Insulation in our hand- and footwear that allowed us to travel free of frostbite in −57°F temperatures.

I also would like to thank our two Major Sponsors, with whom I had the pleasure of working and becoming good friends: Bobbie Sumner with Wells Lamont, who provided John and me with Hotfingers, the best possible handwear we could find; and Julie Staley with Dyneon THV Fluorothermoplastic, who provided viewing windows in our expedition tents that remained flexible during the extreme cold.

I want to thank all the volunteers and friends in my hometown of Grand Marais who spent many hours either in the office or packing the 1,800 pounds of people food and 7,500 pounds of dog food that was to be shipped via icebreaker and Twin Otter airplane to depot locations around the island.

I am grateful to my parents, Jim Dupre and Kate Cartier, for giving me the tools necessary to explore and follow my dreams.

I owe a special word of thanks to First Air and its employees in Canada for the wonderful service to Greenland. Our appreciation goes to Andrew Campbell and Sonja Mabiglia. Our extended thanks go to Greenlandair, Inc., for getting us safely to various locations, in difficult weather conditions, throughout the island. Thanks to Niels Kreutzmann, Sussanne Gunnersen, and Peter Hojgaard Nielsen. Finally, a handshake for a job well done goes to Sigurdur Adalsteinsson and Flugfelag Nordurlands in Iceland for flying all our supply depots to north Greenland.

Thanks to Peter Norton, Mike Hopkins, Cody Shimek, and Simon Norton with RumJungle Media, Inc., for documenting the expedition for us and providing us with the best video equipment possible.

My appreciation goes out to the following individuals who showed John and me their support, hospitality, and knowledge, making this journey more memorable and enjoyable:

United States—Buck Bensen, Mark Hansen, Dick Eckel, Sue Schurke, Mary Ann Atwood, Tom West, Rod Johnson, Chris Vanderheide, John Wood, M.D., Kathryn Frommer, Steven Holz, Linda Zenk, Clark Baldwin, Joel Sheagren, Larry Roepke, Betsy Bowen, Tom Fiero, Tom Healey, Karen Blackburn.

Denmark & Europe—John Anderson, Olrik Vedel, Palle Norit, Hauge Anderson, Niels Jensen, Carine Virwimp.

Greenland— Bent Linaa Jensen, Erik Norskov, Torben Diklev, Søren Lynge, Jens Danielsen, Ono Fliescher, Hans E. Pedersen, Claus Nielsen, Tine Lisby Jensen, Robert Peary II, Oodaq Duneq, Hans Jensen, Jens Carl Jensen, Bent Olsen, Allan Chemnitz, Uilog and Ojstein Slettermark, Poul Hendriksen, Aleqa Hammond, Leong Wai Meng, Vittus Qujaukitsoq, Ove Rosing Olsen, Jan Thrysøe, Captain Fritz Ploug Nielsen, Gert Jakobsen, Hanne Sørensen, Sunneva Caspersen.

Australia—Wynne Hoelscher, Howard Welan, Danny O'Reilly.

SPONSORS

ACR Electronics, Inc.

Advanced Composites, Inc.

Alternative Energy Engineering

ANC (Advanced Nutritional Corp.)

Arctic Umiaq Lines

Aurora (Warm Skin™)

Australian Geographic

Bassett's Meats

Battle Lake Outdoors

Blooming Prairie Whole Foods Co-op

Boreal Access

Boy Scouts of America, Atlanta Troop 463

The Brunton Company

Buck's Hardware Hank

Burett Watches

Caribou Mountaineering

Cascade Kayaks

Clif Bars

Cook County State Bank

CPL (Custom Photo Laboratory)

Crazy Creek Products

Danner Boots

Devold

Dyneon (THV Fluorothermoplastic™) Major Sponsor

Exel Marketing, Inc.—Peltonen skis

Fantastic Foods, Inc.

First Air

Frisby Technologies (ComforTemp™ Insulation) Lead Sponsor

Garmont USA

Gordini USA, Inc.

Gotta Go, Inc.

Granite Gear

Greenlandair, Inc.

Hot Toddy's

Jackson-Mitchell

Kista Arctica

KNI Pilersuisoq

LaCrosse Footwear, Inc.

Lake Superior Trading Post

Land/Shark

Learning Outfitters, Inc.

Midwest Mountaineering

Moss Tents

North House Folk School

North Star Container

Optimus

Pacific Power Batteries

Paddlers Supply Co.

PMI Petzel

Rockwell International

Rollei Cameras

Royal Greenland

Royal Arctic Line A/S

Samsung Opto America, Inc.

Seelye Plastics

Sorensen & Gudbergsens A/S

Southwest Wind Power

Stearns Manufacturing Co.

Swiss Army Brands (Victorinox™ Division) Lead Sponsor

Tasman Sheepskin Tanneries

Tele Greenland A/S

TEXT/plorations

Thor Lo Socks

Toshiba America, Inc.

Traverse Bay Manufacturing, Inc.

Trimble

Walrus Tents

Wells Lamont (Hotfingers™) Major Sponsor

Werner Paddles

Wintergreen Designs

Wronski Veterinary Clinic-Australia

Wynne-Hoelscher Group Australia